MEMOIR
from the
MANIC YEARS

DISCOVERING HUMILITY AS THE ANTIDOTE TO ANXIETY

KIMBERLY ANNE IVERSON

Published by Restoration Media Group
A division of Restoration Studios, Atlanta, Georgia
Edited by Eileen Lass and Jane Gilbert

ISBN: 9798883852656

To request permission, contact the author at: kimberlyscoachingATL@gmail.com

All Andrew Murray quotations taken from the second edition of Murray's Humility, published in London by James Nisbet and Company in 1896. This public domain copy is hosted by the HathiTrust Digital Library (hathitrust.org).

Unless otherwise indicated, Scripture quotations are taken from the ESV® Bible (The Holy Bible, English Standard Version*), copyright © 2001 by Crossway, a publishing ministry of Good News Publishers.
Used by permission. All rights reserved. ESV Text Edition: 2011.

Scriptures marked NIV are from The Holy Bible, New International Version, copyright © 1973, 1978, 1984 by International Bible Society

Although not directly quoted, many concepts and themes draw from Indwelling Life of Christ by Major Ian Thomas copyright © 2006 by Multnomah Books

Many thanks to

Danny Iverson
my husband, friend, and
the one who loved me through the manic years

Peter Jones
whose initial prayers and recommendation
led me to meet Andrew Murray (again)

Betsy Jones
my greatest cheerleader

Dad
humble servant and prayer warrior

Dale and Sandy Hokanson
whose friendship and home were the source
of the closing chapter of these pages

CONTENTS

FORWARD

Life is hard. Ministry is hard. Raising a large family is hard. Doing so while ministering in a low-income community is harder. How to not just survive, but thrive?

Kimberly Anne Iverson has been traveling this path with her husband Danny for two decades, serving in ministry while birthing and nurturing eight (now nine) children. When she writes about dragging herself to Jesus in the midst of manic, frantic demands and responsibilities, we should listen.

Most of us, when faced with overwhelming demands and challenges, like to plan and work our way out of them. Figure it out. Double down. Work harder or smarter or faster. But that's not the gospel. Jesus, save us from ourselves when we do this.

Kimberly points us to another way—the Way, resting in the Way, walking in the Way, working with the Way.

By meditating on Andrew Murray's classic *Humility*, she discovers afresh the grace of God, which saves, satisfies, and sanctifies her in the midst of her overwhelming life. Her whole job, she writes, "is actually experiencing the character of a capable and competent God as he bestows life *into* me... not to prove myself through the things I accomplish or the successes I attempt to secure."

Returning again and again to Murray's insights, she experienced day-by-day transformation. "It took the pressure off. It allowed the wonder to rise. It caused the heart to well with gratitude rather than panic with the pressures of all the logistics and details. And I spoke to those amazing kids more gently because of it. When the pride of living for self was gone, then all that was left was gratitude." She learned to start out the day "dead" (to self) so that Jesus could shine through her.

Don't we all need this? To be constantly reminded that God does powerful things through humble, available, surrendered souls? To be gently led back to our gracious, Forgiving Savior?

Memoir from the Manic Years reminds us that sanctification is not a one-and-done event. Spiritual growth is incremental as we submit ourselves to God and his Word, and obey the prompting of the Holy Spirit. Kimberly's book is like a refreshing visit with a wise, kind friend who points us to Jesus and invites us to repent, believe, and move forward in faith and joy with indwelling Savior.

Maria Garriott
Author of
A Thousand Resurrections
and
Stronger Together

INTRODUCTION

Inside I was a pinball machine of frantic thoughts – so many events and deadlines to keep up with, so many decisions to be made regarding the children, so many home life logistics to maneuver, a ministry to help lead. And it was all intermingled with guilt. The guilt was like the sludge that the pinballs rolled through.

"You really should be gentler with your children."

"You haven't reached out and called that person yet."

"Why are you so stressed out all the time?"

"Why can't you keep up with the housework better?"

"You have such a blessed life – what's wrong with you?"

"If you have Jesus, where's your joy?"

It was three months after having birthed my eighth child and I felt as though I had the weight of the world on my shoulders. No amount of external help from my husband or friends could quiet the internal frantic energy and stress. We had hired someone to come help clean the house twice a month. A family who had moved in with us was helping get laundry folded. I had fairly helpful older children that I could lean into to help around the house. But still the inner storm raged.

Wakeful hours were exhausting ones. Even if I wasn't in an adrenaline rush to get kids to the next event, even if I had a minute to myself or had a slower day with the kids at home, my inner being continued on in overdrive. It was like a tornado I was constantly trying to hold and contain, so I didn't end up exploding... or imploding.

My insightful husband knew I needed to get away for a little while to rest and hit "reset". He pulled so many strings and shouldered extra responsibilities so that I (and my sweet baby) could go to a friend's mountain house for two days. As he drove me up there, I remember telling him, "Honey, I don't know if this will even 'work'. If this is postpartum hormones then no amount of quiet time will silence this inner storm."

I'm so glad he didn't listen to his wife.

I arrived at the cabin, tried to spend time in prayer and reading my Bible, but I was so frantic inside it was hard to focus. I decided to at least try to work through the massive "to-do" list that had been haunting me. I paid bills, worked on insurance issues, made doctor appointments for my husband and children, corresponded about my kids' schooling, added extracurricular activities and school events to the calendar. I was getting as much in place as possible before re-entering into my normal, full life. But the raging inner storm continued. I was desperate for inner peace and rest, but it eluded me.

After a run through the woods (still in an attempt to get out all this nervous energy), I broke down weeping. "Jesus, hold me! Jesus, hold me! I can't hold myself or my life together any more!"

God hears the cries of desperate people.

Within the hour, I came across a little book written a hundred years before my frantic, overwhelming life began. The author was dead and gone, but his truth is one that every generation needs to hear.

"Humility" by Andrew Murray. The minute I heard of it, I was drawn to it.

But what could humility have to do with *anxiety*[1]?

As a matter of fact,

EVERYTHING.

I started the audio book, and within moments of beginning to truly hear its message, I could almost physically feel the pent up anxiety, energy, and tension drain from my body.

I listened to these words reminding me that I was simply a creature in God Almighty's created order. With this, I was reminded that I was created by Him, and therefore completely dependent on Him. I was reminded that I was a corrupt sinner saved from my death-infusing pride by a Savior Who humbled Himself to die

---

[1] Anxiety is a multifaceted issue within each individual who experiences it. Physiological factors such as hormones, brain chemistry, and gut health all affect an individual's experience. This book solely addresses the manner in which mindset shifts and heart-postures affected my personal anxiety journey.

for me, and therefore I was completely dependent on Him. I remembered that this Creator God was the One Who had drawn me to Jesus in the first place, so therefore both I and my faith were completely dependent on Him. Jesus Himself had said, "Apart from Me, you can do nothing." I was therefore completely dependent on Him.

Andrew Murray called out the pride so deeply rooted and imbedded in our hearts. He spoke to how it was actually pride that kept us trying to control things, and kept us hoping in ourselves to manage our lives, defend our reputation, and fight the appearance of weakness. It was pride that kept us resisting, tooth and nail, anything that would cause humbling in our lives.

I was swept up into this glorious moment of repentance and brokenness and freedom and joy and deliverance, all wrapped up in one.

Those century-old words called me out for trying to be god of my life, my family, my schedule, my ministry.

I was set in my place.

A simple creature.

A ransomed traitor.

A follower of the Humble One.

And I found freedom there.

A LITURGY FOR THE READER

If you have never participated in liturgy, I invite you to begin here. A liturgy provides an anchoring prayer and centering as we begin any activity. No matter how flustered our minds are, it gives a place for our thoughts to land and our prayers to emerge. Traditionally, the part in bold is for the facilitator of the liturgy and the italicized part is the response and prayer of the reader. Here, I lead you in a prayer you can pray each time you open these pages to read a new portion. May God answer these prayers beyond your imagination.

Father, you see the readers and already know the burdens and cares they carry as they open the pages of this book. You are able to bring physical, emotional and spiritual relief to those who humble themselves under your goodness and sovereignty.

> *Father, I humble myself- meet me now just*
> *as I am.*
> *Father, reveal Yourself- all that You are.*
> *Father, relieve me now of burdens I was*
> *never meant to carry.*

Prince of Peace, You brought peace because you faced torment when you hung on a Cross. Because of Your sacrifice and

resurrection, may the readers experience Your righteousness and resurrected Life.

> *Jesus, I receive your righteousness now.*
> *Jesus, I receive Your healing power into my body.*
> *Jesus, draw me into union with your Presence and Purpose.*

Holy Spirit, You are the One who leads people into all truth. May You breathe on these pages and blow refreshment and freedom into the hearts of the readers.

> *Holy Spirit, I yield myself to you completely.*
> *Holy Spirit, guide my thoughts and inform my intentions.*
> *Holy Spirit, empower me to walk out the freedom that comes as I live in complete dependence upon You.*

DISCOVERING HUMILITY

How I Became a Student of a Dead Guy

I had been sitting in a hammock, diligently trying to compile my daughter's baby book while I had 36 hours away from seven of the eight precious but oh-so-needy children God had entrusted to me. This was my two-year-old's baby book, mind you – I had already had another child and so it might be time to actually get the toddler's one done. I had been sitting there, still trying to "get ahead of life," while I listened to the free audio recording of Andrew Murray's words as he spoke of humility.

"Humility is perfect quietness of heart.
It is to expect nothing,
to wonder at nothing that is done to me,
to feel nothing done against me....
It is to have a blessed home in the Lord
where I can go in and shut the door,

and kneel to my Father in secret,
and am at peace as in a deep sea of calmness,
when all around and above is trouble."

-Andrew Murray

I kept sorting pictures on my phone. Dragging and pasting and listening.

**"The creature has only to look back to the origin and first beginning of existence,
and acknowledge that it owes everything to God;
its chief care, its highest virtue, its only happiness now and through all eternity.
[The creature's only job] is to present itself an empty vessel,
in which God can dwell
and manifest His power and goodness." (p.3)**

And then,

**"...this grace [humility] is...nothing but that simple consent of the creature to let God be all...
[the creature] surrenders itself to His working alone." (p.10)**

As the words and the reality of them washed over me, I remember the actual physical release that happened in my body. It was as if every bouncing pinball of worry and every ounce of frenetic, anxious energy seemed to drain out of my body through my feet. It was the most freeing feeling, and I wanted to savor the moment. The peace-instilling truth that "I am just a creation of the Almighty God" washed over me and it almost made me want to laugh for joy. "If I'm just one of His creations, I'm ultimately not responsible for anything! If I am simply an object of Someone Else's creative and sustaining energies, then this blessed reality can be my freedom: I am not in control and I was never intended to be!

If I do not even have the power to keep my own heart beating or my own lungs filling with oxygen, then why on earth am I so stressed out about trying to sustain all these other elements of my life?

When I am in the trenches of "normal life," flying from one crisis to another (whether that be a diaper crisis or a sibling bickering crisis or a this-application-form-is-late crisis or someone in the ministry is about to get evicted crisis), it is easy to get sucked into a false reality where I must be the savior and sustainer of all issues within my reach. My head's bent, my mind is focused, and I'm resolved to "fix" or deal with each new issue that comes my way, the faster the better. But here, away from all the hustle, focusing on this blessed reality of nothingness of self as it is dwarfed by the competency and completeness of the Giver of Life, it feels silly to be so absorbed in my own attempts at managing life. As I listened to the words of Mr. Murray, all while continuing to click away at pictures to commemorate my daughter's babyhood, it became clear what was the source of my anxiety: MY PRIDE.

In a day and age where we are instructed to always "believe in ourselves," give ourselves affirmations, and play the victim when life is not going well, it is ironic to have found such freedom in having a dead guy tell me that all my troubles were actually rooted in ME. But this is the gift of repentance.

Repentance is actually naming the sin- the source of our stress and unrest- so that it can be confessed and surrendered. All the self-help I had attempted just left me more defeated and discouraged. *What if the best help I could give myself is receiving this rebuke: that the pride of my heart was what was causing me to work so hard at all the self-help attempts? What if it was my pride that kept me trying so hard to keep it all together? What if it was my pride that caused so much anxiety when I was late for so many appointments, missed so many emails, or sheepishly opened my messy home to so many individuals?* The anxiety to keep it all together was actually pride in my reputation. The strain to keep everything going and keep "on top of life" was actually pride in believing that I was competent and that my abilities were enough. The burdens over my children's behavior, education, and disabilities were really my pride not wanting to "fail" as a mom.

Murray's words had unearthed it all:

"Humility is perfect quietness of heart. It is to expect nothing [of ourselves], to wonder at nothing that is done to me, to feel nothing done against me. It is to be at rest when nobody praises me, and when I am blamed or despised. It is to have a blessed home in the Lord where I can go in and shut the door, and kneel to my Father in secret, and am at peace as in a deep sea of calmness, when all around and above is trouble."

Humility was to need no outside approval, as long as the secret place with the Father was preserved. Humility was to have everything wrapped up in the magnitude of Who God is.

What if all those burdens I was trying to juggle could be thrown into the abyss of God's competency? If I am just dust brought to life by the breath of God, then of course I can't keep all those parts of my life sustained! There is only One Who sustains all things, and His name is Jesus. Hebrews 1:13 tells us that He upholds the universe by the word of His power. Living under the pretense that I actually could keep up and keep things together was both exhausting and disappointing.

What if, with each failure and embarrassment, I just said,

"Yup, Failure's all I've got to offer.." ?

What if I named it before I could be embarrassed by it? It would definitely take the pressure off to meet others' expectations of me. The title "failure" could not be freeing if it was done with self-condemnation and self-loathing. No, the deep disappointment in myself was only rooted in the prideful belief that I could or should produce anything other than failure.

What if I owned the fact that I was insufficient, with a gaze on the horizon knowing that the Son of righteousness would rise with healing in His wings, and for all my incompetencies, He will ultimately be the Hero and Sustainer of my life?

What if my admission to being a failure was actually a simple admission that I will always be a failure at fulfilling God's job, which is complete perfection?

What if I looked beyond my abilities with a confidence in the grace of God to cleanse, fill, sustain and empower weak, failing people, all so His glory and goodness could be made more visible?

My time away from my family had come to an end, and I was on the drive back home. Home to messes and schedules and needs and the full-force franticness of "real" life. I had experienced a full twenty-four hours of complete release and peace after my hammock revelation. But now that I was returning, I could feel the stirrings of anxiety arising. *How could I hang on to the peace, the trust, the calm that had come with a gaze fixed wholly on the competency of God with no thought of my own abilities? How could I maintain this trust while I have a thousand things coming at me all at once?*

Confessing and forsaking pride seemed an easier way of life than maintaining my fight to keep up my reputation, my self-dignity, and my own management-of-life skills. At all costs, I would pursue the humility that would be the doorway into this blessed life. I wanted this blessed life, not simply for the sake of ease, but because on the lowly road of humility I would find, over and over again the meek and lowly Lamb of God. And where He is, peace is, because He is the Prince of Peace.

There were only two resolutions that came to me on that drive home. First, I would listen to Andrew Murray's words about humility over and over. I needed his coaching through the future challenges I would face, for the welcoming of humbling was such a foreign concept to the natural, prideful inclinations of my heart. Second, I would start my days out on my face. Most days when attempting to do things in my own strength I would end up falling flat on my face relationally, emotionally, or spiritually anyways, so if I started my day out on my face literally, it would be a physical reminder of where I should start and where I will end, if not rising in the strength and power of the ever-present Christ.

As I mulled over this virtue of humility, I would jot down what I was learning. All my cute journals had been apprehended by six-year-old aspiring artists. Instead, I grabbed a discarded black and white composition book. You know how overly zealous teachers require the purchase of hundreds of dollars of school supplies and then only use half of them? Yeah, I found one of those with my son's name marked off the front because he only used the first page of it.

The rest of this memoir is the rehashing of how, in a fight for my sanity and my freedom, I sought to allow this message of humility to permeate my days. These days would be full of the same endless tasks and responsibilities as a mom of eight children that I had before the revelation. They would be days filled with the continued requirements of a hostess, youth mentor, and urban ministry partner. But these could be days lived out with a massive paradigm shift.

This book is indeed a memoir written during those manic years of being vastly outnumbered by our children: a newborn, toddlers, a dyslexic kindergartener, elementary kids and young teens. They were years filled with parenting and all the tasks, schedules, issues, and emotional needs of each child. Throughout this time, I simply had a black and white composition notebook that became my holding place for thoughts and the processing of this humility concept. Humility, as it applied to my real-life inward and outward struggles. Those writings occurred in the nooks and crannies of life-while kids played on playground equipment, while waiting during tutoring sessions, in the first few moments during nap times, or during the late night unwinding after I (finally) got kids to bed.

The format of this book is similar to what I had jotted down in that composition notebook. Some entries are long, some are short. I write not as an expert imparting truths to her pupil; it is rather the pupil rewriting her lessons so that the truths might stick. It was the cheat sheet for keeping mind and heart in check for the next challenge.

The writing of this account was an attempt to learn this lesson of forsaking my all-encompassing pride, losing my own agenda, and walking in the humility of "blessed nothingness."

I could lose my pride, or else I might lose everything that I ever found dear in this life.

As you read this book, remember its title. It is a memoir – a historical account of the principle of humility being pulsed into the biography of my years with young children, middle children and teen children. It was written in the manic years. Manic means "full of activity, excitement and stress; behaving in a busy, excited, anxious way" (Oxford Learners Dictionaries) (If anyone told you raising this many kids was anything but manic...they'd be lying.) The manic years are those when I had so many littles, and so many snotty noses, poopy diapers, temper tantrums, joyfully made messes, creative destruction, and emotional whirlwinds of teens and preteens, all while living in an inner-city setting supporting a husband in more than full-time ministry serving people.

Finding bits and pieces of time to sit down and process what I had been learning was hit or miss, and this writing reflects that. If you want a fully-organized systematic teaching on humility, I suggest reading Andrew Murray's own words (although you will find many of his quotes throughout this work), or The Blessing of Humility by Jerry Bridges or The Freedom of Self-Forgetfulness by Tim Keller. If you are up for the wild ride of exploring humility as it plays out in an overloaded mom and inner city pastor's wife, keep reading.

Why so many fonts?

One to capture my discourse about humility.

One to capture my self-talk throughout the stories.

One to capture all of Andrew Murray's direct quotes from his book on humility.

One to capture direct verses from the Bible, handwritten just like on all of my crumpled index cards and notebook where I wrote so many of the verses out as a lifeline.

Talk to Me, Mr. Murray

When I first started listening to Andrew Murray's book about humility, he was not a complete stranger to me. I had stumbled upon his writings years earlier as I sought to grow in my prayer life. I remembered reading one of his introductions that he had written his book on prayer while on a ship traveling between his preaching engagements. It had made such an impression on me that he could write a short book on a ship and it the book could endure far beyond his lifespan. If he could write such a powerful book on a boat, which wouldt impact me hundreds of years later, it might be worth imperfectly embarking on my own writing career. This had led to the publication of my first book *Heirloom, The Faith and Wisdom of Anne Murphy* two years before this current frantic state in which I found myself. His life and writings from the mid-1800s had been pertinent to my prayer life and faith walk. Now, as I was exposed to yet another of his writings, I would find that humility would be key in my deliverance from anxiety in the 21st century.

Up to this point in my life, I knew humility was a good thing, but I didn't realize how crucial it was to my peace of mind and my walk with God. Largely, "humility" had been something I walked in when I was feeling miserably defeated by my sin struggles and the constant awareness that I just couldn't "get it right" along the way. Little did I know the dejected mood masked as humility actually stemmed from my prideful belief that I could somehow have possibly done any better (more on this later). I also had no idea that *before* the utter defeat of sin struggles, humility could be the doorway into handling situations in a way that actually honored God as I lived in a state of blessed nothingness. I surely didn't know how blessed and peace-filled I could be as I went about my life pursuing this virtue.

But in that hammock-swinging, ear-filling and heart-piercing state I grabbed hold of every word of Murray's and let it ruminate in my being. The overview of this short book, *Humility*, which may or may not have been written on a ship...but more likely was written on his face before the Lord, is as follows:

Chapters 1 and 2

First, we see that humility is actually the glory of the creature. To be created is to be designed to live in dependence on one's Creator. To live in dependence on and therefore fellowship with the Being who brought life from dust and breathed breath into lungs, is to be free and functioning as we were designed to function. The fallen angel, who through the pride of his heart brought about his own downfall, seeks to lure us into that same pride and cause our defeat. Pride always leads to defeat. Humility always leads to exaltation. Satan, in all his prideful self-will seeks to elevate our importance and undermine our dependence on God so that he can repeatedly cause the fall of man to replay in our lives, relationships, and communities (Gen.3). Humility, though, is the secret of redemption. It was in the humility of Christ Jesus (Who left heaven to become a lowly human, housed in dust that He Himself had created) that we were redeemed from this fallen state of pride. The very root of Christ's life is *humility.* For us to walk any other path is to walk a path void of Christ. Jesus gave up all honor of men to seek an honor that comes from God alone. When we live into the same reality and pursuit, it gives freedom from the opinions of those around us for the sake of just One opinion.

Chapters 3, 4 and 5

While on earth, Jesus consistently spoke of the blessed nothingness of humility, which was ultimately the source of His power. He lived and taught humility and throughout His discipleship of the Twelve, He was continually redirecting them into this life of dependence. None of the disciples walked in true empowerment by the Holy Spirit until they went through specific experiences and failures that caused them to realize that their only power and wisdom would come from above. With the ascension of Jesus after His death and resurrection and the subsequent Pentecost, Jesus' followers were finally in a state where they could be led and empowered by their Creator, through the Holy Spirit. This was "a returning" to the pre-fallen state that Adam and Eve had briefly experienced. By the infilling of the Holy Spirit, once again man could enjoy intimate fellowship with and dependence on the God of all, the Lord Almighty Himself.

Chapters 6

True humility impacts our relationships, our daily attitudes, and the general trajectory of our lives. In the Epistles (letters to the early house churches) the Apostle Paul repeatedly instructs how the early believers in Jesus were to conduct themselves... in humility.

"Honor one another above yourselves" (Romans 12:10 NIV)

"Love does not envy or boast, it is not arrogant (prideful) or rude." (I Corinthians 13:4)

"Walk with all humility and gentleness...bearing with one another in love" (Eph 4:1b,2)

"Do nothing from selfish ambition or conceit, but in humility count others more significant than yourselves." (Philippians 2:3)

Humility towards God can only be measured by the degree of humility towards those around us. The holiness that many earnest religious people desire actually manifests to the degree that humility gets self out of the way so that God's holiness is allowed to dwell in the individual.

Chapters 7, 8 and 9

Humility influences our relationship with sin, but not necessarily through the continual confession of our sins, past and present. Rather, humility leads to the confession of our keen awareness of being a hot mess (my words inserted, not Murray's) apart from a moment-by-moment dependence on God's abiding grace. Unless this grace continues to uphold us, we will end up functioning in our fallen state and attempting to do life for God apart from God. Murray goes on to expound on Jesus' words in John 5:44,

"How can you believe, when you receive glory from one another and do not seek the glory that comes from the only God?"

Here we see that seeking the glory of this life is linked to unbelief and unbelief is lack of faith. Humility, though, is actually the root of true faith. If we still seek and love and jealously guard the glory of this life (the honor and reputation that comes from men) then there is no room for God to have and be all the glory. Faith in its most elemental state is actually the confession of nothingness and helplessness, the surrender and waiting to *let God work* (Ch.9,29)

Chapter 10

Jesus' life lived to the glory of God alone led Him down the path of death. If we are to experience any fullness from fellowship with Christ, we will walk the humble road of death to self in a thousand small experiences, becoming a servant of all just as He was. Murray beckons believers into the death and life of Jesus, calling all to humble themselves and descend each day into the grave of perfect, helpless dependence on God. The result will be a resurrected life. That resurrection brings freedom and peace. When a person moves from fearing, fleeing from and seeking deliverance from all that can humble him and rather embraces weakness and humiliation as a doorway into fellowship with Jesus, then freedom can occur. No circumstance can then rock one's inward peace because nothing-no set of circumstances-can hinder the enjoyment of the Prince of Peace Himself Who dwells within a humbled heart.

Chapter 11 and 12

Finally, humility leads to exaltation, but not necessarily exaltation by men. Once humility has worked its way into the human heart, the praise of men cannot satisfy one's deepest longing. The exaltation that humility brings is not necessarily the success of powerful prayers and deliverance from circumstances that strain the body and soul. No, the exaltation that humility brings is a rising above one's circumstances, above others' opinions, and above even self's opinions about oneself. In the humbling, the glory of God has room to manifest and unfold in a person's life, causing a continual heart feast to occur. In the humbling and surrender to

God, one is exalted to an immovable state of peace and security that is based on nothing but the steadfastness of God Himself.

In closing, Murray admonishes the reader to engage in a continuous prayer:

Great and glorious God, in Your goodness reveal and remove every form and kind of pride in my heart, no matter the source-whether from Satan or my own fallen nature. Awaken in me a humility that enters into nothingness in the depth of my being so that all of Your Light, Glory and Holy Spirit may enter in. May I reject every thought except that of waiting and praying for Your grace that leads to humility – the humility to live a life of continuous surrender. Jesus I am nothing. Jesus, here I am. Be ALL in me.

Amen.

It is nice to read these ideas in a book, but how does one practice humility in the *now*? The remainder of this book will be the account of praying and pulsing these realities into daily life and existence.

Talk to Me, Jesus; An Overview of Christ's Life of Humility

"I have come down from heaven, not to do My own will but the will of Him ho sent Me."

John 6:38

If Andrew Murray had discovered the quietness of heart that accompanies humility, he wasn't the one to think it up himself. He saw it in the life of Jesus, Who humbled Himself and had no agenda but the Father's. Up there at that mountain house, as I listened to the *Humility* audiobook, I discovered how humility was actually the key to Jesus' peace, trust and subsequent eternal impact on all of history.

It is ironic that the day I planned to sit and write out all the ways Jesus surrendered His agenda for the Father's, nothing on *my* agenda went right.

The week prior, I had shoved a leftover door (yes, an entire closet door) into my van all because of my minimalistic ambitions to get rid of all of our leftover home renovation supplies. Well, that stupid door slid forward when I slammed on the brakes. (I can't imagine why I was going so fast?!?) It busted my windshield and broke my air conditioning and heating fan on impact and needed to be fixed. So I had planned to drop one set of kids off at school, swing by and drop off a different set of kids to preschool, drop off the car to the autoshop and then walk to a coffee shop to spend the next three hours writing. Except all this happened on the one day in April that the wind chill was 37 degrees. And the one day the wifi didn't work at the coffee shop. And the one day my computer wouldn't charge because a kid dropped it on its edge. And the one day that the exterminator called to tell me we had a mouse problem. And the one day that leaking shower back at home with the moldy crumbling tiles couldn't be addressed because I forgot to grab pictures to send to the mold guy, who was waiting for them before we could move forward in fixing it. Then there were the simmerings of frustration over my teen who wouldn't, for the life of him, actually do the chores I kept asking him to do. Add in the guilt over my irritation and sharp tones with him and my other kids. Under all these normal life pressures, I had this nagging reminder that I had neglected my morning time of prayer and surrender for the sake of a few more snooze buttons.

I wanted to just start crying in that freezing cold while I walked to the computer repair place. All this precious, wasted time-without-kids. How on earth could humility have anything to do with a day of cold frustrations and pricey repairs?

Maybe everything.

I was on my third cup of coffee. (I had felt obligated to buy some-thing from every local fast food shop I had visited to find a warm, plug-available spot for my frustrated writing endeavor that morn-ing.) As I typed, I let Jesus talk to me despite the caffeine jitters.

> *"If anyone would come after Me, let him deny himself and take*
> *up his cross and follow Me. For whoever would save his life] will*
> *lose it, but whoever loses his life for My sake will find it."*
> *Matthew 16:24-25*

My kids and I had spent our morning commute praying for family members who had moved to a third world country and were fac-ing insurmountable obstacles and hardships. They were clearly humbling themselves, denying themselves and taking up their crosses. How could I also deny myself living this comparably cushy comfortable life— a life that still frustrated me? I decided to keep letting Jesus talk to me. I skimmed through Murray's entire listing of how Jesus did life.

"Truly, truly I say to you, the Son can do nothing of His own accord, but only what He sees the Father doing." John 5:19

"I can do nothing on My own.... I seek not My own will but the will of Him ho sent Me." John 5:30

"I do not receive glory from people." John 4:21

"I have not come to do My own will"... John 5:30

"My teaching is not Mine..." John 7:16

"I have not come of My own accord." John 7:28

"I do nothing of My own authority." John 8:28

"I have not come of My own accord, but He sent Me." John 8:42

"I do not seek My own glory." John 8:50

"I do not speak on My own authority." John 14:10

"And the word that you hear is not Mine." John 14:24

Over and over again, He states that He is not about Himself. Here it is, the Savior of the world, the King of creation, and He **has no agenda**. He was on a mission of complete surrender and yielded-ness to the will of Another. It says it right there in Phillipians also:

"though He was in the form of God, did not count equality with God a thing to be grasped, but emptied hHmself, by taking the form of a servant,...he humbled Himself by becoming obedient to the point of death, even death on a cross."
Phillipians 2: 6-8

Maybe it was my agenda, albeit a seemingly good one, that was causing such frustration? Jesus, Who was God Himself, chose to empty Himself and take on the role of a servant. The Man Who had no agenda, Who was emptied and obedient, ended up accomplishing an eternally significant agenda. He saved the entire world from their rightful punishment, gave them new hearts, and then rose to be King of kings Who lives with His people through His Spirit. That's an intensely productive life. All the things that were happening that cold morning were so frustrating *because* I had an agenda, a productive agenda. Maybe the emptied and obedient life led not only to an emotional, physical and spiritual release like I had in my hammock experience, but also led to a *more* productive life, an eternally productive life.

Jesus said it over and over again: He was nothing, He was emptied of Himself, He didn't try to accomplish His will. Heck, He didn't even speak His own words, He said. He had surrendered His will completely. With that surrender, He walked in perfect trust of His Father, which led to perfect peace and joy. It was a peace and joy and confidence that would draw people to Himself. He knew His Father, He was hearing from Him, and others were drawn to that connection to the Almighty. This union led to a nonstop schedule with people's needs continually coming at Him. (At least that part sounded familiar to my life with eight kids, but somehow His schedule didn't affect Him the way mine flustered me!)

Jesus navigated all of life in this broken, busy world with a complete denial of personal agenda and the loss of self. The only way I could proceed forward would be functioning in that same state. After all, grasping at all the items of my agenda – a working house, a working car, a working computer, working relationships – had just left me frustrated, defeated and feeling out of control.

But I was never in control in the first place.

So what if, like Jesus, I started there? What if I surrendered my control, my will, my agenda, and my words to the Father, believing that a sovereign Lord was ultimately over all the unfoldings of my life? What if the more frustrating the circumstance, the more graciously God was wrenching from my grip the illusion that I could control anything at all? If this were true, all the messages that pulled at me through social media, society around me, and even "American Christianity" were actually part of an illusion of control that would never, ever materialize, no matter what new program, purchase or plan I attempted.

Where would surrendering control and yielding to God lead, though? Jesus walked the road of surrender and it led to the ugly, torturous shamefulness of the cross. But I know it also ultimately led to resurrection. Maybe that is where I would find hope, find *Him!* In the past I had tasted how peaceful and sweet His presence was, so if I took the road He took, I might find fellowship with Him there. The cross might be the crossroads of intersecting His life and mine.

I had already experienced the frustration and angst that comes with the preservation of *my* self and *my* will. To join Jesus in the humility of the cross would be to make space for third-day resurrection power. A supernatural intervention. Personal death to self would give God the opportunity to work whenever and however He wanted, and *His* works do not disappoint.

There was only one way to proceed forward while staying engaged with all that was before me as a busy mom: the death of self. Not the death of me as a human (there was still too much to live for!), but rather the death of my inner self ambition. The self, or inner rumblings of who I am that rise up and demand my way, my timeline, my convenience, my comfort. Children happen to be the greatest catalyst for threatening that inner drive. And I happened to have eight of them. That's a lot of opportunities for my inner will to die. But *if* that part of me died, the anxious, I-need-to-manage-every-little-detail-of-my-life would die as well. What if I, or that inner self, showed up to every circumstance... *dead*? Dead people can't have problems. Dead people can't get frustrated. They actually lead a fairly uneventful and peaceful existence. What if the taking up of my cross and walking towards the death of self was the very key to the peace my anxious heart craved?

To fight for life would be to fight in futility.

To lower in humility, would be to live in liberty.

As I dug into the Bible, I saw it even more throughout Scriptures:

He denied Himself, surrendered *and was at rest.*

"You will keep in perfect peace those whose minds are steadfast, because they trust in You." Isaiah 26:3 NIV

He denied Himself, surrendered and endured the cross.

("He endured the cross, despising its shame ..." Hebrews"12:2)

He denied Himself, surrendered and conquered death.

"Christ has been raised from the dead,...the last enemy to be destroyed is death. For "od has put all things in subjection under his feet..." Corinthians 15:20, 26,27

He denied Himself, surrendered and became the Redeemer of all humanity.

"Christ Jesus, Who has become for us wisdom from God—that is, our righteousness, holiness and redemption......" 1 Corinthians 1:30

That's a pretty successful and productive life.

There might be something to this life of humility – and not just the long term end goal of it, but rather life in the midst of it.

Murray sums it up well,

"If humility be the first, the all-including grace of the life of Jesus,-if humility be the secret of His atonement, then the health and strength of our spiritual life will entirely depend upon our putting this grace first too, and making humility the chief thing we admire in Him, the chief thing

**we ask of Him, the one thing for which we sacrifice all else."
(Humility, p.7)**

But we seek out humility not for the sake of obtaining a virtue. No, humility is not an end in itself. Rather, it is the doorway into an intimacy and fellowship that can be the energizing joy and strength for our lives.

"I want to know Christ and the power of His resurrection and **the fellowship** *of His sufferings, being conformed to Him in His death" Philipians 3:10 BSB*

In the midst of dying there would be a fellowship with the One Who walked that road before us. If I could get HIM in the process of broken cars and wasted time and frozen fingers, then I would come out on the other side the winner. Just like He came out of the tomb having won us for Himself.

And what does dying to self in the midst of parenting and ministry and grief and triumphs look like? I determined to find out...and record the journey in the process.

chapter 2

WHO'S IN CHARGE? HUMILITY TOWARDS GOD AS HIS CREATURE

There is an amazing freedom that comes with the humility to gaze on one's Creator and know He is God and we are not. To truly believe, *"I am just one tiny part of His expansive creation"* means He is ultimately in charge and we were never meant to be (in charge). This is actually a blessing! As God has to teach and reteach our hearts to remain in this posture of the mind and heart, He uses the most mundane of circumstances to do so. In this chapter we will look at the ways our circumstances can bring us back to the reality of Who is in charge.

The Most Important Job

It is dizzying. All the needs. The squabbles. The logistics. The laundry. The housework. The number of messes that explorative little hands are able to create at exponential rates while I frantically try to clean up the previous one....all while the day's actual to-do list lies untouched on the counter.

It often feels like someone more organized and capable should have this job.

Mothering eight children is not for the faint of heart.

After a frazzling morning of homeschool, I load kids into the car, take them to green spaces and I run to clear my mind. As my body moves and fresh air is breathed, I hit "play"on my Humility audiobook once more. The words I listen to start to join my fractured and frazzled soul with Elmers glue (the same stuff caked to my kitchen table). It serves to connect the fissures and recenter me on what I was really made to be. My thoughts swirl: *Is it the ministry with so many needy people and so many potential ways of serving them? Is it the homeschooling efforts? Is it the health coaching business that requires quite a bit of extra time on social media? Is it listening to podcasts about the productivity program I long to implement in an effort to outrun and "beat" this frazzled feeling?* This particular morning has me thinking that if I could just work at something and feel successful, then I could feel at peace. I was buying the lie that productivity could replace personhood.

Well, the words I listen to leave all those swirling thoughts obsolete in comparison to the radical (to me) state that I am being called into. Andrew Murray's words through that little Humility audiobook tell me to get lower, to forget self, to abandon the pride of ambition and enter into the humility of dependence and surrender.

As I listen, I am reminded of who I am based on Who made me and why, instead of trying to create who I am based on what I can accomplish or prove.

"When God created the universe, it was with the one object of making the creature partaker of His perfection and blessedness…communicating to them as much of His own goodness and glory as they were capable of receiving…but the relation of the creature to God could only be of unceasing absolute, universal dependence. (Chapter 1, pg 3)

Wait a second. If God's aim in making me was so that I might share HIS perfection and HIS blessedness, then the pressure to create my own perfection and blessedness is taken off my shoulders. My very existence is an invitation into the partaking of the fullness of His good character. If I fully allow this reality to settle into my being, then it means that I could stop striving and straining to be successful on my own terms. The only striving would be to live in a state unceasing dependence on my Creator and Savior.

I keep listening. As I run my laps around the playground, I'm relieved that the kids are still fully occupied with climbing and playing. I have a few more moments to get my bearings again.

"The life God bestows is imparted not once and for all, but each moment, continuously, by the unceasing operation of His mighty power." (Ch.1, pg 3)

The life *God bestows*…Sort of like the new creation I am promised to be if I am in Christ (2 Corinthians 5:17). The life God wants for us is a life that is given, not achieved. It is a life that is to continuously come from the Giver of life, rather than a life we grab hold of and then try to live independently.

What this means is that my whole "job" is actually the job of experiencing the character of a capable and competent God as He bestows life *into* me. My job is not to prove myself through the things I accomplish or the successes I attempt to secure. I, as a creature, am entrusted with various roles and responsibilities that often seem too overwhelming and difficult. But what if they aren't actually up to me? What if they are just invitations into emptiness and dependence? If this is the case, then an enormous amount of pressure and anxiety is released from my state of being. This truth means that the only job I need to excel at is one of presenting myself as an empty vessel for Him to work through.

"But we have this treasure in jars of clay, **to show that the surpassing power belongs to God and not to us."** *2 Corinthians 4:7*

If my earthen "clayness," or incapability of holding everything together, shows off God's power as He works in me and through me, then all of those overwhelming, frustrating and humbling circumstances seem to be an opportunity rather than a setback.

The more overwhelmed I am, the more incapable I realize I am – which sooner or later will cause me to humble myself and surrender, presenting myself to be the emptied vessel. The more my circumstances say "you can't…cant' keep up, can't get it right, can't hold it all together, the more I have to look outside myself for answers and aid from the One Who **can.**

Isn't this what humility is? Getting the focus off of self, so Another could have the spotlight? In this case, the spotlight goes to the only One worthy of it – the Maker and Sustainer Himself. The sooner I come to the end of myself – my pride, my self-will, my agenda, my efforts (even if they are efforts towards good things) – the sooner my incapabilities will lead me to the supernatural power where my deliverance is found. If humility was the road that led Jesus to be the Redemption of all mankind, then humility in my daily living would lead to my own redemption as well.

How does a person resolve to walk in humility? How do you pursue humility without allowing pride to propel the pursuit? How do you go about walking in a life of humility the way Jesus did, the way the Scriptures described? I knew there needed to be an emptying of self...but then what? And how?

I remember back to those first few weeks after my revelation at the cabin – the weeks when I first walked in awe and wonder of how humility played the most integral role in experiencing peace. Those weeks were not completely void of the panic and anxiety that had threatened to suffocate me, but rather weeks of gentle releases that kept my eyes fully on God. Those weeks had me running frequently into my room to get physically on my face again and again and again to deposit the anxiety when it started to well up inside. As I looked to Him, my gaze was diverted away from my own abilities (or lack thereof) and back on to the One Who did have the ability to handle my full family and ministry life.

In different interludes during my day, I would prostrate myself on the ground (this was the lowest position I could physically obtain, and humility is about lowering oneself, so doing it physically served as a good reminder to my soul). Then I would declare, sometimes for the 17th time in the day "I can't do this. I am nothing. You are all." I would then envision the Lord Almighty Who was the first Being to think up families and motherhood and Who had sustained billions of mothers in generations past. And I would pray to Him,

"I lower myself before You.
Have Your way in me.
Have Your way in this home.
I can't, but You can."

I would emerge from this 2-3 minute ritual choosing to believe that He truly had it all. Then I would just show up in the chaos – the messy kitchen, the meals needing preparing, the school papers needing organizing, or the doctors' appointments needing to be scheduled – knowing I wasn't the one ultimately responsible for it all. Those first few weeks almost felt like an out-of-body experience.

With each wave of anxiety, my coping methods were those face-plants and declarations. As I went through my day, I kept telling myself the script of the story.

"You are just a blip in God's created order (for some reason I felt such solace in remembering how tiny and ultimately insignificant I was). He keeps the earth spinning, the planets orbiting, the seasons changing, and it goes on as it has since the beginning. For generations before me, God has brought forth individuals and families to

live and prosper and develop on the earth. He is good at running the show. He watches over the deeds of mankind, He even inserted Himself into mankind to redeem them. He worked justification, He worked resurrection, He worked salvation. He works the renewal of all things. If He has done all this and continues to do so, He doesn't technically need me."

I remember how amazing it was once the revelation of my insignificance came to the forefront – it made me laugh, for the sheer lightness of it all. I was not in charge! I was not sustaining anything! It allowed me to revel in the fact that I could have breath in my lungs and blood in my veins. ("I get to be here?!?!") I was getting to experience all of creation, including all of these eight children that I was privileged to mother. None of all this is ultimately up to me – it is just an experience that a good and all-sufficient God was allowing me to experience. I imagined all the significant and important things my children would grow to accomplish and I was amazed that the Creator would insert me into this part of their stories. It was almost as if I was merely an observer as I participated in my life. It took the pressure off. It allowed the wonder to rise. It caused my heart to swell with gratitude rather than panic with the pressures of all the logistics and details. And I spoke to those amazing kids more gently because of it. When the pride of living for self was gone, then all that was left was gratitude.

It was joy inducing – this road of simply emptying self, so that God could be all, and fill all, just like it said in Ephesians 1:23 (NIV)

"God...appointed Him [Jesus] to be head
over everything for the church,

which is His body, the fullness of
Him Who fills everything in every way.,"

Maybe the ambition to accomplish more and get my life more under control was simply a dead-end road, or a circular pathway. What if my most important job was the availability that the emptying of self brought? What if my most important job was to get out of the way so that the God of the universe could do His most important job – His work of "abundant redemption"? (Psalm 130:7)

A kid starts bellowing because of an ant bite. I calm the child, fishing an ice cube out of my water bottle to numb the bite. My chance to exercise is over, but I ponder it all.

Abundant redemption.

Oh, how we need that! I want that abundance for my family and so desperately for myself!

I beckon everyone to load back into the van. I am met with several calls for "Just one more, Mommy" but finally I wrangle every-one into the van. As we drive off, I leave with a single-hearted ambition.

If I was never successful at any other job – managing my home, co-ordinating schedules, parenting, missionary endeavors, running side businesses – may I be successful at this one thing: surrender. May I pursue the humility-induced surrender that gives God space to be God in my life. I am beginning to see, to really believe that…

When given the space, God does powerful things through imper-fect, but available lives.

The Love of Christ Sits Me Down

"You prepare a table before me in the presence of my enemies." Psalm 23:5

"The love of Christ constrains me." 2 Corinthians 5:14

I'm driving my car (always so much driving!). As I sit, my mind races ahead to all the things I didn't get done today. Races ahead to how I'm going to have to get so many balls rolling the minute I walk through the door: the kids' homework, putting the bill payment in the mail, unloading groceries, responding to school emails, and starting dinner. Races ahead to the laundry that didn't do itself today, the homeschool lessons that are half done, the messes left on the floor, the lawn that will never stay "kept", the ministry clothing donations that are still sitting in the living room unorganized. I am like a racecar revving my engine at the starting line as I anticipate racing forward to try to beat the incessant to-do list that haunts me, chases me and tells me that if I could just hurry up and get things done then I would finally experience *rest*.

As I stop at stop lights, I recite Psalm 23 out loud in a desperate attempt to calm the inner engine in hyperdrive. The words "He prepares a table before me in the presence of my enemies" roll over my lips, and a picture emerges. The Lord has me sitting, and His arms are holding me in place. I'm not sitting at a steering wheel, but at a banquet feast. Instead of sitting to enjoy the meal, I am trying to hop up and get busy rearranging the table set before me in order to reconfigure the place setting and direct the meal the way I think it should unfold.

I realize what the Holy Spirit is trying to show me in the moment. Conviction sets in. I am always trying to rearrange the life, the moments, the people set before me. This often manifests itself in the form of irritation with my kids – the barking bossy mom voice full of commands void of love or kindness. These kids keep interrupting my plans, or messing up our physical spaces, or failing to be fully-capable-adults-in-tiny-bodies-who-don't-constantly-need-something-from-me. (Go figure!) Well, why wouldn't I want to rearrange all that?!? But this discontentment with the current arrangement also manifests itself in a complaining tongue, a depressed spirit and continual grumbling about what *isn't* right in my life. And it makes me and everyone around me miserable.

As I drive, the "He" in the verse stands out to me. He prepares the table. The place setting is thought through. It is made ready. He sets it down there intentionally.

Am I willing to accept and receive the table that He sets? Am I willing to trust and allow Him to be the all-knowing and good Shepherd that Scriptures say He is? And more importantly, am I willing to surrender myself to Him in whatever role He has placed me? Even if it is encourager of whining kids, or steady laborer with too much to do, or peacemaker amongst sibling bickering, or helper in ministry events, or confidant and prayer warrior for inner-city neighborhood struggles?

Humility allows me to be in those roles, with those sets of circumstances, without my peace changing based on the outcomes.

I remember back to when I had heard Andrew Murray coach me while doing laundry one day. (The *Humility* audiobook played in the background of my life as I toted my phone around the house.) He spoke of every annoyance and every grievance as a humbling to be welcomed. *Even this mountain of laundry? Even the reoccurring messes that could be prevented if I had just trained my children better? Even the mundane tasks that feel like a waste of my college-educated brain?*

Murray says that if God opposes the proud and gives grace to the humble, then with every humbling circumstance I would find grace given there. If humiliation was where grace was found, then my attitude could shift to delighting in those humbling circumstances rather than being repulsed by them.

The reason I could give thanks in even unwanted circumstances is because the humbling ones are those that connect us to the Humble One. This is indeed a grace. I toss a stray sock into the dryer. What a freeing, mindblowing thought! What if rest wasn't in a life of arranging things the way we want them, a laundry-free existence? Maybe joy wasn't in the *absence* of the humbling and frustrating situations but firmly planted with Christ *in the midst* of them? If true rest was actually found in allowing any set of circumstances to be placed before me without trying to jump in to change it, crouching on the laundry room floor might be a place of feasting.

Anxiety will not be such an effective bully when I am trusting that a Sovereign God is in the place setting.

We arrive home, with so many moving parts, moving bodies, moving emotions and moving temperaments. We walk in the door heavy laden with all the items from the day's activities in our arms. Before I even dive into the chaos all around me to try to order it and rearrange it, I step over stray shoes and apple cores and sneak into my room for some "face-plant parenting." I literally get on my face to surrender and to declare truth to myself. I surrender to the living Lord Jesus Who has the power to move in me this evening, and I declare out loud (in order to help my spiritual amnesia) that I trust God for the exact scenario, and the exact table that He sets before me. It takes me less than five minutes. How much damage can the herd of kids stomping into the house do in that amount of time?

Evidently a lot. But those quick moments of humbling myself before the Lord reset my mind and heart to walk back into it all. As I go about the action packed evening, I am in an internal mindset of sitting at the table of intimacy with my Savior. The table is set in the presence of my "enemies". And believe me, there are alot of them. Physical messes, relational messes, schoolwork, ethics messes, attitude messes all pose as enemies, trying to kill joy and rob me of contentment. But tonight there is a table set before me, and I am will dine at it.

The mighty hand of God can tend to all the details, and I will offer up myself as a willing participant. The details that these hands of mine may tend to, or that these lips may speak into, or that these ears might listen to, are actually details that *He deals with through me*. As I accept the table set before me with a heart of surrender, I am being compelled and constrained by the living Jesus each moment as He does the work through me.

I do not need to reset this table.

My heart simply needs to be reset.

Now I can allow the love of Christ to sit me down to enjoy the feast.

"You prepare a table before me in the presence of my enemies." Psalm 23:5

Be Still and Know It:
"There Is No Shortcut to Me"

I had just knelt down beside my bed, the little humility book laid open before me. I had set my phone timer for twelve minutes. I needed to meet with God and meet quickly. Too many other things loomed over my thinking. But the minute my knees hit the ground, the gentle rebuke came.

"There is no shortcut to Me."

The reality of those words begin to penetrate my soul. There is no way around it. Jesus wants me to sit and dine with Him. I can't have a "Jesus on the go." The only way of abiding is in stillness. When Scripture speaks of the tree that is planted by streams of water, it is just that...*planted*. A staying. A state of remaining connected. And the only way there can be an inward "staying" throughout a day of full (or frantic?) activity is if there had been a physical, mental and spiritual staying through *stillness*. I must start with stillness.

It is humbling to still myself. When the pressures and demands of my day seem so looming and large, and I feel like I am the only one who can tend to them, then I am driven on by them. *But is it the tasks that drive me on, or is it a large view of myself and a small view of God's almighty power?* In my nearsighted and prideful view, I think that I can outrun and outrace the clock and accomplish the millions of tasks. Oh, the humility to let God be God! My stopping to behold Him will never stop the world from revolving, the planets from orbiting, nor my family from functioning. He truly does "sustain all things." (Hebrews 1:3) In the stopping, I don't declare my finiteness just with my mouth, I declare it with my whole body, down to every muscle. Stillness. Before I entered the world, all things continued. After I leave the world, all things will still continue.

I hear loud noises downstairs. Stomping of feet. My body tenses. *Do I trust a risen Christ to hold all things together in my home? His Word says that He holds all things together by the word of His power. (Colossians 1:17) Can He do it now, during my scheduled prayer time?* I could sprint down there in a panic, yell at my kids to settle down, and then complain to God that I can't even get twelve minutes to slip away and be still with Him! Too many times, this is how I have dealt with this type of situation. This time I stay. I have to say it out loud: "I trust You, God, with whatever is going on downstairs." I keep praying through the prayer verses I have written out. I wait until my phone timer goes off to go downstairs. I choose with my will to believe that the God Who was *with* me at my bedside is also *in* me as I return to the kitchen.

The floors are covered with granola that the three year old spilled. I choose to believe that the Spirit Who raised Jesus from the dead is living in me to clean up the mess and to look children in the eyes and be a voice of calm instead of a voice of panicked anger (Romans 8:11). I have humbled myself out of this situation so that He can be the one reacting, interacting, and working to tend to whatever needs are presented.[2] I find that the only way my heart and mind can have the stillness to let Him behave through me, is if I have been physically still. In the little stops in my day, I get the chance to recenter, recalibrate and to undizzy myself from the spinning of life. When I stop to pray, worship or listen, I am telling my body that only God is God. My body can, in turn, remind my brain that there is room to be still and know that He is God if I simply give Him the time and space to act.

I start sweeping granola. I look my children in the eye. I envision Jesus, the servant leader, bending down to sweep up the mess. I welcome the chance to serve curious small people. I thank God for the chance to mop parts of my kitchen that would not otherwise be mopped that day. My frantic energies can sustain nothing. His powerful energy can sustain all things. But the only way I can tap into that sustaining power is if I cease and desist so that He has room to enter and empower. There is no shortcut to Him and ironically, to avoid attempting a shortcut, I need to be still. Yes,

---

[2] Concept largely drawn from the teachings of Major Ian Thomas, author of The Indwelling Life of Christ

"I will be still and know that He is God" (Psalm 46:10), even while sweeping granola.

The Humility of Stillness

My brilliant husband thought of it. The coronavirus outbreak had canceled our East Coast trek, but after prayer we found ourselves at a borrowed timeshare in beautiful, sunny Florida. Six children ago, we stopped calling our family trips "family vacations." Trips with that many people were in no way vacations. We chose to call them "family memory-building trips" instead.

Until.

Until my strategic husband thought of the idea of getting a cheap hotel (usually on priceline) for two nights so that each of us parents could get a vacation from vacation. While one parent manned kids at the pool, the other would get away for 24 hours to sleep, watch movies, bask in the sun, or whatever they wanted to do. Then we would tag team and the other would get a turn.

Usually if I ever got time away from the very full life with eight kids, I came with an enormous and overly hopeful to-do list of "fun" things for me to do. Bible study. Reading a parenting book. Exercise. Correspondence with loved ones. Working on my health coaching business that was turning out to be more of a hobby than a part-time job. Making baby photo albums (there was always the newest child's book that I hadn't quite tackled yet). There was always so much to catch up on. An urgent "now's your only chance!" nagged me during any times without the constant needs of my children. Sometimes the nagging urgency to make the most of the time ended up rendering my "alone time" even more mentally stressful than being swept up into the immediacy of all of my kids' needs.

On this particular vacation, as soon as I knew that I would be getting 24 hours, the mental to-do list began whirling around my brain. A still, small voice spoke into the gathering storm: "Come with no agenda". As my husband drove me over to the hotel, he said "Honey, I just want you to rest while you are away. Just rest." Then on a phone conversation and prayer time with my brother, he said, "Kimberly, can I just challenge you to not try to get anything done?" I settled in and headed to the fitness center and a random song interjected between the smooth jazz..

"Take this moment to be STILL.

The world is spinning 1000 miles per hour.

Let's just take this time to be still."

What?! Even the gym radio is telling me to do this?? I was ready to surrender to the now-not-so-subtle promptings of the Lord. After my workout, I wrote down the swirling, hopeful to-do list so that it had a way to exit my brain. I laid it out on that hotel bed and entrusted it to the Creator and Sustainer God Who keeps the world spinning 1,000 miles per hour (and keeps it from spinning out of control, I might add). I handed it over to Him and chose instead to wait on Him.

And it was hard.

It was difficult to be still.

It was somewhat agonizing not to be checking my phone, posting pictures of our lives, or catching up on mom stuff.

Could I really just wait for the Lord?

Could I wait…not for strength to mother, or inspiration to write, or help for managing my business, but just wait?

Wait for *Him.*

Because of HIM.

Because His presence is ultimately the only thing that can ever satisfy, or ever calm me, or ever hold me.

His presence was the only thing that could keep me from getting overwhelmed, anxious and frantic (and subsequently angry) once I would be reunited with my kids. His presence would be the only thing that could sustain me when I got back to the grind of juggling a full family and ministry life. But if I couldn't tap into His presence right here in the stillness, then I certainly wouldn't be able to when I had eight kids needing me.

So I started to practice it in prayer. I didn't even tap into my enormous prayer list for my children. I just pressed into Him for *me.* It took me a few hours to slow my race-ahead mindset down to be present *with* my body, to be present *with* Him. It's not that I didn't do anything. I went for a walk. Went and got ice. Took a shower. Journaled some Scripture. I just did it *with* Him. And I did it in expectation.

"I lift up my eyes to You, to You Whose throne is in heaven.

As the eyes of the servants look to the hand of their master,

As the eyes of a maid look to the hand of her mistress,

So [my] eyes look to the Lord my God until He shows [me] His mercy."
Psalm 123:2

Could I go twenty-four hours with only ONE pursuit? To simply want more of Jesus? Just Him? Not even intercession for the things that burden my heart and the many spiritual, mental and physical needs of my children, neighbors and ministry?

Could I blockade all mental bombardment for twenty-four hours?

Do nothing. Yes, to fast from activity, which can sometimes be deadlier to the soul than gluttony of food is to the body.

The idea to set a timer for twelve minutes to just pray popped into my mind.

Then a timer of eight minutes to just worship and adore. It wasn't a legalistic endeavor, not a formula, but rather because, as a physical human in a frantic and physical world, I needed time markers to act as little eye shields and blinders to keep me focused. I needed minutes passed by to keep my mind and body and heart in one place – a place of expectation and longing for one thing.

Be still and know.

"Be still and know that He is God." Psalm 46:10

To hear the Father's heartbeat.

To let my own heart get back in rhythm with His.

The only path to thriving would be once the heart had stopped and been realigned to the cadence of the Father's. There could be no frantic striving *to it*, simply a resting and relaxing *in it*.

The Humility to Settle for Less

To gaze on Jesus Christ, God made flesh, is to gaze on the ultimate example of accepting and settling for....less. Jesus chose to humble Himself and live in a human body, in human history, in humanity's dwelling place. He chose limits. He chose to leave the omnipresent state of heavenly rule. As Jesus functioned in the confinement of a human body, He taught us the real way to be human and the real way to function as a creature of the almighty God.

Humanity. The humility to be human.

If Jesus chose it, could I also submit to it?

In settling for less, and in abdicating the "right to rule," Christ ended up gaining for us so much more than what just His rule alone could accomplish. His ability to look past the frantic of the immediate and focus on the all-knowing Father's will, led to accomplishing far more than One human body could accomplish in its limited foresight. He trusted the foresight of the Father, and obeyed every prompting the Father gave Him. He had the humility to see less (in the earthly sense) so that He could hear more (of the Father's heart). In humility, and in settling for less, His obedience and surrender brought about the saving of the world from their sin. Juxtapose this with all my striving for more, and one can see He chose the more effective route. Who knew humility could lead to more productivity?

I am notorious for always attempting to cram too much into too little of a time window (which is precisely why I am late all the time).

Who knew that at the very root of that is... PRIDE?

Yes, there is a lot of service involved in the tasks at hand. There are eight kids' lives dependent on me to help them survive or not flunk out of school or not kill each other when they get in fights. I have to get all this housework accomplished. I have all these people and these ministries to serve in. But pride expects more and holds the highest of standards in the process. The pride of my heart says that I should be able to seamlessly work at the speed of light without any interruptions or mishaps, and therefore **I will**. I will, whether it overworks me, over-stresses me, or over-frustrates me to the point of my hurting or neglecting those who are nearest and dearest to me. Pride puts an unrealistic expectation on how much one brain, one one body, and one set of 24 hours can produce.

What if I had the humility to recognize that I, and those around me, are simply finite beings that live in utter constant dependence on their Creator? What if I learned to function as such? What if, as a dependent creation, I gave space to the Creator and Sustainer to get His will done, rather than always striving to get mine done? What if I gave allowance for my entire family to simply be creatures that have bodies that need to sleep and eat and be still and not even think at times? Perhaps accepting the finiteness of myself and those around me is in itself an act of humbling. Perhaps it is even an act of worship that gives glory to God for being God, possibly more so than all the ministry events. Accepting the smallness of being one tiny aspect of God's created order might be the doorway to freedom. It would replace the extra stress I bring on myself when I glorify my own capabilities through unrealistic expectations. Humbling myself could eradicate the anxiety that overcommitment brings on me.

All of the drive for more comes to the crashing forefront each time I have gotten pregnant. I will have dreams, ambitions and ministry and homelife goals, and then, just as the locomotive is revving its engine to barrel forward, it comes to a screeching halt. The frame cannot keep up with the heart it holds. But all that ambition, even ambition for good things and for serving others, can still be rooted in the pride of self that has a drive to conquer. The seeming "setback" of physical limitation (whether it be pregnancy or illness or cancer diagnosis) might actually be the humbling that saves the soul. Christ's attitude of abdication flies in the face of this ambition.

Christ showed us that He could be the powerhouse that changed the course of humanity (and eternity) all while walking in complete humility. The very act of entering creation as a Baby was the climax of paradox. The King of all turning to become subject to all. In His state of confinement (to a human body) He looked continually to His Heavenly Father and lived in dependence on Him for His every move. The things He spoke were not "I've got to, because I rule..." but rather statements that basically said, "I'm not in charge." When Jesus said to His disciples,

"The Son can do nothing of Himself, but only what He sees His Father doing" (John 5:19)

and then again,

"I can do nothing of My own." (John 5:30)

He was abdicating autonomy.

He declared that He was not carrying out His own agenda and plan but had completely yielded to the Father and His plans.

"I have come down...not to do My own will but the will of Him ho sent Me." (John 6:38)

In doing so, He accomplished more than any human who had ever lived – the redemption of all mankind, thus changing the entire course of history.

He settled for "less" and achieved so much more.

chapter 3

WHO'S SAVING WHOM?: HUMILITY AS A REDEEMED SINNER

Grab Hold of the Altar

I had been fasting in the New Year. With the fast was a desire to detox from all the rush, the sugar and junk food, the late nights, the stress, the angry outbursts and irritations over how messy, or chaotic or loud or tardy things were becoming in our home. I was getting back into the habit of getting on my knees when I first got home from my full days. Granted, this hitting of my knees was not because of some holy ambition. No, it was because, by that time in the day, after running around with kids, I was tired. In order to plow through the homework, the evening chores, the dinner-making with subsequent eating explosions, and the bedtime routines, I was desperate for empowerment from the Almighty. Otherwise, another ugly mean mom outburst would ensue.

It was in that state – on my knees with my face pressed against the floor – that the sense came.

"Grab hold of the horns of the altar."

What an odd instruction.

It brought to mind the Scripture I had read a few weeks prior when reading 1 Kings 1 and 2.

A man who was guilty of death for treason, betrayal and power-grabbing was about to receive the consequences for his behavior. Another man who was guilty of shedding innocent blood was about to receive his just punishment. In both instances they ran into the Tabernacle in order to obtain mercy and have their judgment pass over them.

The horns were on the Israelite altar of sacrifice inside the Tabernacle, the place of worship and intercession for the people. It was the place where the blood of innocent animals was shed so that the judgment that the people of the land deserved would not fall on them.

Figuratively, the Holy Spirit was telling me to grab hold of those horns of the altar in this modern age while trying to raise a modern family. Lord knows, I had been guilty of those same things the men of 1 Kings had been. Power-grabbing and controlling my children in an attempt to control my life – a job only God could rightfully do. In the process, I had engaged in my own version of shedding innocent blood. As a mom fighting for control at every turn, I admitted that the tender hearts and minds of my children had often been the bloodied victims of my fight for power.

I, a guilty mom, was now in need of the blood sacrifice of the altar – except it wasn't a physical altar in a Tabernacle in ancient Hebrew history. Rather, it was the altar of Christ's sacrifice on the cross. Just as the men of 1 Kings needed mercy extended to them based on the sacrifice on the altar, I was in desperate need for mercy to be extended towards me based on Christ's death for my life. The consequences of my aspirations to "be like God" (Genesis 3:5) needed to be covered by Christ's sin-absorbing blood. I needed those horns and that sacrifice and that mercy, not just for past sins but for present moments: every moment. It was that sacrifice that won for me the right to have fellowship with the Father, despite still being wooed by the prideful self who demanded her way. There was only one mercy, and one Savior and one merciful God who was strong enough to manage the ever-ballooning prideful self.

The Balloon

It indeed is like an inflated balloon.

Pride.

Andrew Murray wrote,

"And so pride, or the loss of humility, is the root of every sin and evil. It was when the now fallen angels began to look upon themselves with self-complacency that they were led to disobedience and were cast down from the light of heaven into outer darkness. It was when the serpent breathed the poison of his pride, the desire to be as God, into the hearts of our first parents that they too fell....[throughout the ages]

pride, self-exaltation, is the gate and the birth and the curse of hell." (Chapter 1, pg 3)

It was the inflation of self that led to the fall of Satan, an angel who desired to be worshiped and acknowledged like God. It was the inflation of self (Adam) that led to the eating of forbidden fruit, following the lie that to be more and to accomplish more, one had to do it independently from communion with God.

It was the inflation of self that caused the whole hellish unfoldings of a fallen world.

And it is the inflation of self that causes hellish things to happen in my household.

What could the remedy be for such conflict and struggle?

Murray continues,

"For this is the great truth that lies between the fire and pride of fallen angels, and the humility of the Lamb of God--that evil can have no beginning but from pride, and no end but from humility." (paraphrase mine)

As I sought the type of humility that led to the infilling salvation of Christ, I found myself to be like a balloon filled with air.

I could squeeze it on one side – in ministry "humility" or in "humility towards my neighbors," but then it would just inflate itself in another area of my life – in parenting or home-tending. It was like that balloon that still had air in it....no matter how you squeezed, it would always bubble up in a different spot.

What I needed was to be completely emptied, presenting myself as a deflated balloon with no air left in it. There had to be nothing competing with the new breath that God desired to breathe into it. Then and only then could another motive, another presence, another power be able to fill it.

It was exactly as Murray had told me.

"The truth is this. Pride may die in you, or nothing of heaven can live in you." (Note A, pg. 5)

God was inviting me into a choice. There would need to be an active choosing between one or the other. There could be either absolute emptiness, in the loss of agenda and power, or absolute pride, in the striving to be and do what I wanted. Only one infilling of the balloon could remain. Would it be the fullness of self? Or the Infilling of Christ through His Spirit in me?

Jesus is not in the business of doctoring up dead things. No, He's in the business of whole new creations (Galatians 2:20, 2 Corinthians 5:17). He's not in the business of changing people, but exchanging their lives for His. He's not trying to make dead things look like they're alive. Wasn't this the whole point of prompting me to "grab the horns of the altar," to be reminded of the death sacrifice that Jesus made for me once and for all? And be reminded that, in order to experience Christ, I must climb on the altar myself? If humility is the loss of self, then to gain new life, HIS life, there must be replacement of the old. This is what it means to be a redeemed sinner, not a renovated one.

When He beckons people to Himself, He is calling them to death.

"If anyone would come after me, let him deny himself and take up his cross daily and follow Me." Luke 9:23

"I have been crucified with Christ. It is no longer I who live, but Christ who lives in me." Galatians 2:20

Pride makes the old self want to stay alive, occupy space in the balloon and is willing to do all kinds of good, even Christian deeds, to try to stay in the balloon. But Christ first models and then calls us to come and die. He wants emptied vessels, not just vessels that have made a little bit of space for Him. This is what it means to be a *redeemed* sinner. God in His kindness will allow me over and over again to come to the end of myself so that this glorious reality might pulse through my daily life.

"And you were dead in the trespasses and sins....But God...even when we were dead in our trespasses, made us alive together with Christ." Ephesians 2:1, 4a, 5a

The Glory of the Wrecking Ball

*"If I must boast, I will boast of the things that show my weakness."
2 Corinthians 11:30*

A wrecking ball comes through my home; it shatters the peace, sending slivers of discontentment, fear, shame and powerless-ness. It crushes relationships and barrels through trust. Fear and confusion are smeared across the faces of the children who reside there.

The wrecking ball is me.

It has been months and months since I had experienced a 24-hour getaway, weeks and weeks since I had any semblance of a Sabbath. I was running on fumes from our frantic schedule, our jam-packed weekends. We had a deaf woman with many health complications and her mentally impaired grown daughter living with us temporarily. What we thought would have been two weeks had turned into six weeks, with no progress towards obtaining a permanent home for them. I found myself caring for ten human beings, not including my husband, instead of just eight. On top of exhaustion came the onslaught of disrespect and talking back by most, if not all, of my kids. A jam-packed schedule does not lend itself to the patience and consistency that parenting requires. So some very poor communication habits had slipped into our relationships.

On top of the fullness of our home life, we had put on a giant ministry worship night which was a Spirit-filled and powerful time. But it also meant returning home with all the kids at 2:00 am. We woke up the next morning to scramble around to get our home ready for house church. Again it was a wonderful time of prayer and ministry. Some folks lingered, so I quickly made lunch to feed my crew plus the stragglers. As we finished up fellowship (which was rich and wonderful), the boys from the community played basketball in our driveway. Our guests, whom I had just fed, were saying goodbye and one of them said offhand,

"Alright, I'm going to go home and *relax* now."

I smiled and waved goodbye, but inwardly I burned with jealousy. Instead of rest, I had the mountain of the afternoon's tasks looming: a kitchen that needed to get cleaned up after feeding so many; ten children (my own plus the extra ones staying with us for the weekend) to wrangle into afternoon responsibilities before our full week started again; laundry to do so school uniforms would be available; kids to prod into getting their homework done; little ones to put down for naps.

When will I ever get the chance to rest?

I get to work, and mid-laundry transfer, I find that my exhausted husband had drifted off to sleep upstairs.

Unfortunately, that brief nap didn't last long.

All it took was some smart alec comments in response to my request to stop the basketball game in order to come in and do homework. The frustrations began to fume in me. Then there was the grumbling about needing to read, and a teenager angrily complaining about having to help clear the counter -- like I was the most unreasonable monster to ask for help after having fed everyone. I went upstairs to find a teen zoning out on her phone and another child having stolen fruit snacks from my closet (my ONLY off-limits spot to stash future treats for the kids).

All the exhaustion and powerlessness over what seemed like an endless, grueling, never-stopping schedule welled up.

In utter and complete rage.

I threw something across the room and I started screaming at everyone. The child who stole. The kid who was on her phone. By this time, I marched downstairs to recruit children to help and found yet another kid on a screen. I picked up the small monitor and threw it on the ground intentionally breaking it. "This will be the last time you come down here and sneak screens!" I enunciated as I made sure the monitor was good and broken.

"We have RULES in this house!" I bellowed.

"We don't do screens on Sundays! We don't sneak stuff out of mom's closet! We don't sneak off after meals when we are supposed to be doing our chores! We don't complain when mom asks us to do something! We actually help around the house! If ya'll don't want to listen to me, I will just leave. Y'all don't give a crap what I say anyways! I will NOT be disrespected like this. Y'all figure it out yourself if you hate having a mom asking you to do stuff all the time!"

The wrecking ball swinging through the home was having some effect. Some cried, some scurried to finally scoop up clean laundry out of the laundry room that I had already asked three times earlier in the day to be removed. The counter had at least gotten wiped down.

"I'm done with this and I'm not putting up with this kind of disrespect anymore!"

I shed my church clothes for a tanktop and shorts, scooped up my laptop, journal and some books and got in the car and drove off.

Are you feeling better about your parenting yet? You might also have a list of podcasts I should listen to about actually training children to do chores, instead of nagging them into it, but for the intent of *this* book (not a parenting one), I will proceed...

I had just artfully exemplified Galatians 5:19a, 20b, 21a,c

"Now the works of the flesh are evident...
enmity, strife, jealousy, fits of anger, rivalries, dissensions, divisions...I
warn you, as I warned you before, that those who do such things will
not inherit the kingdom of God."

After two hours of sitting in the warm sun in a field of green, reading a book and dozing off at times, the reality of what I had just done started to sink in. The anger and rage started to blend with shame and condemnation....and fear.

Fear welled up. Fear that this wrecking ball would shatter my children and my relationships with them beyond repair. Fear of losing control again. Fear over how detrimental all this was, especially for my younger ones who didn't do anything to prompt this insane explosion but were still witnesses to it.

I met up with my husband later in the evening. My pride, still too puffed up to back down on my threat, went with me. He carried with him notes from the kids apologizing for disrespecting, for complaining, for stealing, and for sneaking. He told me he would let me get away for a little while if I needed to. I jumped at the offer. I was still so broken and raw, and angry and guilty and exhausted, I didn't even care about all that he would need to rearrange in order to make time for me to rest. After returning home to put the youngest kids to bed, and making sure the elementary kids had their uniforms for the next day, I dashed off to a cheap hotel...and proceeded to sleep for thirteen hours straight.

Exhaustion never lends itself to good parenting. Sleep deprivation never aids in attempts at crucifying the flesh. Sleep loss is not the same as the loss of self found in humility.

Surprisingly, when I looked up "synonym to sleep deprivation" on google, this was the first thing I that popped up:

"A form of psychological torture inflicted by depriving the victim of sleep. Synonyms: torture; torturing."

Well, I had certainly kicked into the part of my brain fighting for survival as it was indeed being tortured with exhaustion.

The Humility to Rest

While I lay there in clean sheets that I hadn't had to wash, I randomly opened to an Old Testament passage. It just "happened" to be about God's judgment on His people due to the lack of keeping Sabbath. I read words written thousands of years ago while I lay there curled up, body still achingly tired and heart still ridden with guilt, but maybe those ancient passages were applicable to right now.

"What is this evil thing that you are doing, profaning the Sabbath day? Did not your fathers act in this way, and did not our God bring all this disaster on us and on this city?" Nehemiah 13:18

Some fairly intense judgments and disciplines came on the ancient Hebrew people. What I found myself reading was actually a warning about what happens when we don't have the humility to rest. God took this Sabbath thing seriously. Could the disaster of the afternoon be linked to the Sabbath, just like the disaster Nehemiah speaks of? Swinging through my home and my relationships like a wrecking ball had certainly gotten my attention. I think back to a verse Murray had quoted often in his book.

"A man's pride brings him low,
But a man of lowly spirit gains honor."
Proverbs 29:22

I guess the wreckage had gotten me exactly where He wanted me.

It had broken me. It had humbled me. And now, here I was, teachable.

I looked up some more passages on Sabbath while in that curled up, resting state.

First, God modeled it.

"By the seventh day God completed His work which He had done, and He rested on the seventh day from all His work which He had done. Then

God blessed the seventh day and sanctified it, because in it He rested from all His work which God had created and made." Genesis 2:2-3

Then He commanded it.

Remember the Sabbath day by keeping it holy. Six days you shall labor and do all your work, but the seventh day is a Sabbath to the LORD your God, on which you must not do any work. Exodus 20:8-10

Then He promised joy and acceptance in keeping it:

"Everyone who keeps the Sabbath and does not profane it,
    and holds fast My covenant—
these I will bring to My holy mountain,
    and make them joyful in My house of prayer;
their burnt offerings and their sacrifices
    will be accepted on My altar;
for My house shall be called a house of prayer
    for all peoples."Isaiah 56:5-6

And He rebuked and corrected concerning it.

"'Hear the word of the Lord... This is what the Lord says: Be careful not to carry a load on the Sabbath day or bring it through the gates of Jerusalem...or do any work on the Sabbath, but keep the Sabbath day holy, as I commanded your ancestors.

Yet they did not listen or pay attention; they were stiff-necked and would not listen or respond to discipline. But if you are careful to obey *me, declares the Lord, and bring no load through the gates of this city on the Sabbath, but keep the Sabbath day holy by not doing any work on it... People will come ....bringing burnt offerings and sacrifices, grain offerings and incense, and bringing thank offerings to the house of the Lord." Jeremiah 17:20-24;26*

Sabbath[3] was a time of physical rest, and God thought it was pretty important. He Himself practiced it, commanded it, spoke often about it, and promised good because of it. If the God of the universe, running this whole show, put importance on it, then nothing but the root of pride had overridden His command. Only pride over the importance of my own to-do list, my own ministry ambition, my own running endlessly around to please my children and meet all their needs could keep me living in disregard for something He so highly regarded.

To stop, to rest, to reflect, to listen: it is a sign of humility. God built into our weekly schedule a consistent reminder that we as creatures need to rest. We are housed in weak human bodies which are prone to fatigue. This very fact reminds us that we are subject to, dependent on, and owing our loyalty towards the Sustaining One. If we don't listen to His commands about Sabbath, sooner or later our bodies will be aching for it, and our emotions will be screaming for it.

Oh, for the humility to practice this physical and spiritual reminder of our finiteness...*before* the wrecking ball swings through the home!

---

[3] *The emphasis on Sabbath throughout Scripture also points to the Sabbath rest that Christ provides for us in His completion of salvation. For the purposes of this part of the chapter, these vital-to-salvation New Testament references are omitted.*

Humility as We Relate to Sins
of the Past and Present

Fast-forward through the following 24 hours (my husband gave me another night to finish recouping). I spent time in the Word. Spent time resting. Spent time connecting with friends. Spent time writing...a book about humility. The biggest monster of all, writing a book about humility. Oh, the irony, or maybe intention, of that scenario.

How could humility have played a role in preventing the insane outburst? I racked my mind for how things could have played out differently had I been walking in an attitude of humility. I knew I had landed on one component of it: the humility to keep the Sabbath and remember the finiteness of the human body I dwelled in. But there had to be more.

It was hard to seek to humble myself when I was still seething with anger at my kids. There was an idealized view of what humility felt and looked like. That idea of humility collided with all the different aspects of the anger I felt. There was the tired anger. There was anger over my inconvenience. There was anger over the ways my children's actions would drive me to such an ugly display of depravity, thus exposing my shame. But there was also an element of righteous anger at the disobedience and disrespect when I knew how much I sacrificed and did to serve those kids. It truly "wasn't right" for my kids to treat their parents as they were, for God Himself tells our children to honor and obey their parents.

Whatever the source, the balloon of pride and anger had nearly burst.

As I wrestled with this, I was invited into a thought:

What if the wreckage gets me where He wants me? What if the parenting disaster that had just happened, including all the splintering of relationships, would and could actually be worked together for good, as Romans 8:28 promises?

I would be willing to be there - be broken in that place- if God could bring beauty from the ashes. If what emerged was a more grace-dependent individual wowed by the extravagant and patient love of a redeeming God, then the wrecking ball and all its damage could be used for good. If my kids witnessed their mother, in the midst of the wreckage, falling into the unearned grace of God found in the forgiveness of Christ and others, then they may learn to fall back into that same source of love and forgiveness. I wanted them to learn this mighty grace lesson, but when and how could the grace lesson penetrate my own life before all the damage happened?

I had been at this "humility hunt" for long enough to know that in the moment of the heated parenting and in the middle of the crisis, slapping a "Just humble yourself" on the situation could not bring about the transformative parenting that I desired. No, the humility and the blessedness that came with it would happen in the preemptive measures. Choosing humility could not be simply an "apply brakes" to a mounting anger and rage session. It was a state of being, not a band-aid to apply to each broken situation.

Andrew Murray gives me clues to the preemptive "saving" that comes from a consistent state of living as a humbled sinner. The saving grace of humility was different from a "saving" found in quickly grabbing hold of a virtue that is supposed to help me in a crisis moment.

When Murray reflects on the Apostle Paul's claim to be "the least of the apostles, unworthy to be called an apostle," (1 Corinthians 10:9) and "the least of all the saints," (Ephesians 3:8), he sees that this claim is not because of current sinning or present sins but because of an overwhelming sense of wholistic sin in oneself apart from salvation in Christ. The claims come in juxtaposition to the depth of grace that would rescue him from an entirely depraved state of being. The Apostle Paul actually lends himself to speaking very little of current struggles but very often of how undeserving he was. His awe of salvation and his claim to being the very least stem from the humility of knowing just how deep of a sinner he was and how powerful a ransom had brought him out of it.

Murray says that we could never be anything other than ransomed sinners. God's child cannot live in the full light of His love unless he acknowledges the darkness of his inner rebellion from which he has been saved. He even goes so far as to say that the only right we have to all that grace has promised to do in our lives is through the claim of "failure," or "prideful sinner." (Maybe even the claim "wrecking ball.") If we attempt to obtain grace with any merit of our own, we immediately forfeit the joy of extravagant grace God extends. The only currency God accepts in order to give out His grace, is nothing. It is the failure-surrender-receiver state of being that joyfully declares, "I've got nothing to offer in this redemption story!"

Paul's (and our) remembrance of having sinned so terribly in the past, and the consciousness of being kept from present sinning, was coupled with the abiding remembrance of the dark hidden power of sin and pride — ever ready to come in. This darkness could only be kept out by the presence and the power of the indwelling Christ." (Ch. 8, pg 27)

Paul declares, "I know that nothing good dwells in me, that is, in my flesh. For I have the desire to do what is right, but not the ability to carry it out" (Romans 7:18). This is not a declaration of defeat and "Why bother?" Rather it is a battle cry on how desperately the indwelling Christ was needed to walk in continuous victory over prideful self.

Paul's humility was actually his doorway to victory. If he knew that every moment that he depended on himself to produce good, he would just produce evil, then a new strategy must be employed. He himself would have nothing to do with it, except to declare his inability. His only hope would be "Christ in me, the hope of glory." An entirely different Hero and Victor! An ever-living and ever-present source of strength!

The glory of goodness, kindness and patience could not emerge from me as a mother trying harder to exhibit Christ to her kids. It couldn't emerge from the mighty apostle Paul who endured so much to follow Christ. No, the goodness, kindness, patience and endurance of Christ could only be exhibited by Christ Himself. And He would exhibit it in me, moment by moment, as my pride got out of the way so that He could have His way. This revelatory moment (or moments) came with the understanding that any effort to be and do good by my own strength were evidences of pride. Pride is the inflation of self. Humility was the emptying of self so that the mighty and good One could be Who He is through me, as I am.

The prevention of the wrecking ball couldn't happen through the last-minute wrangling of the anger. No, the prevention of spinning out of control would be *losing* control in the millions of moments of my day, so that another strength could be dealing with the stresses, or the kids' disrespect or the simple frustrations that *He in me* faced. Another strength could be handling the old power-hungry self that would want to rear up and take control. The prevention of the wrecking ball is *Christ in me*, the hope of glory (Colossians 1:27). And it took me *being* the wrecking ball to come to the revelation of this hope. I had to see my great need to be reminded of how greatly He meets it.

But still, what to do with an anger continuing to eat away at my soul?

I came home just an hour before the kids would get home from school. As I reacclimated from "my Sabbath," I got a few things ready before it would be "full steam ahead" that evening. I started the laundry which had rapidly accumulated in my absence. I unpacked my things. In that empty house I still felt the echo of residual anger burning. I didn't know what to do with it and I knew I wasn't capable of wrangling it.

Well, the next few moments, Jesus showed up and encountered me. He met me in the most intimate of ways to deal with the most intricate of emotions. In my raw, helpless-in-myself state, He gave me a tangible event to reiterate the reality that "apart from Me you can do nothing" and Christ in me, [my only] hope of glory. (John 15:15, Colossians 1:27)

As I folded and sorted clothes, it was as if I could feel two hands reach down into my heart, and take hold of that burning ball of righteous anger over the ungratefulness and disrespect of my children. Those two hands lifted it out of me. The anger was removed from me.

But that wasn't all.

I could see it getting put into the very heart of Christ —-Christ as He hung, stretched out on a cross – disrespected, unappreciated, abused, and absorbing the consequence of every sin of humankind. He was lifting the anger out of me. He was placing it in His own heart. That anger was rupturing His own heart, on my behalf.

I don't know if it would have been enough to only feel it lifted out of me. If so, I think I would have taken hold of it again, or nursed it back to a blaze when the next stressful or frustrating situation with the kids arose. No, when I saw it actually enter into the heart of a Savior who had only known purity and peace, I knew I could never retrieve it. The consequence and the hell of that burning anger was absorbed into the infinite God Who hung, in humility, on one of Rome's most gruesome forms of torturous execution. It was crucified with Christ on the cross (Galatians 2:20). It would be forever absorbed into him. And every little flickering or relighting of the flame of anger would cause this mental picture to arise again: His heart bursting with that anger, His side pierced, blood and water spilling from His dead, crucified body. (John 19:34)

I was in awe of the grace of this encounter.

I was broken by His sacrifice.

And I was ready.

Ready to re-enter the busy schedule, to re-enter into parenting toddlers to teenagers, to face the pressures of our lives.

Ready to have Jesus Himself, reach into the recesses of my sinful heart, scoop out all my justified and unjustified anger and absorb it into His own heart.

Ready for His heart for my children and my community to be placed in mine.

But I was only ready to the degree that I was ready to be emptied of myself. I could only enter back into my life as a completely depleted balloon, ready for the Breath of Life to inflate me. I was ready to walk dependently on the Saving Presence of Christ in me, that would deliver me from myself in the moments, not just in the monumental.

Seeking to walk humbly before my God (Micah 6:8) would affect the schedules and the commitments and the Sabbath keeping. Complete dependence would redirect how much I thought I could handle as just one human being. Humility would shift the view that my children were burdens to be managed. Instead, it would usher in the view that my children are humans I am privileged to engage with and therefore, gifts. But there was more to how humility would affect me. It was only in humility that I could receive the saving grace of Christ. Only in humility could I see just how great a sinner I was and just how much I needed Christ in.every.moment. Humility meant needing Him in each mundane moment, not just the monumental ones.

This was the key to living out humility in the now.

And it was the only way for this former wrecking ball to move forward...through a humble walk – with an ever present King.

chapter 4

A PAIN IN THE NECK: HUMILITY IN OUR CIRCUMSTANCES

When the Circumstances Look Too Overwhelming

A full weekend of hospitality and ministry events left me dragging and dropping. Dragging children out the door and then dropping "all the things" needed from the last event in piles in the house. And this happened on repeat throughout the weekend. There had been many seasons where all the dragging and dropping would have left me completely overwhelmed, spiraling me into screaming sessions at all the little bodies that helped contribute to all the messes (and weren't helping me clean them up).

But this time, truth and lessons from past experiences girded my brain and mouth. Previously, I would have wanted to explode from the sheer overwhelm from the clutter and exhaustion. *What if humility in this situation looked like permission to be human?* Tiredness is allowed to set in. Clutter is allowed to accumulate. A house is allowed to get messy during busy seasons. My children are allowed to just be kids in the midst of it all. Could the bold faith that believed in the all-sufficiency of Jesus for those big ministry events all weekend, also be a bold faith to believe that He would similarly show up right here as I wearily stand over a sink full of dirty dishes? Both forms of showing up require faith and trust. I glance up at a water-splattered note card with Jeremiah 17:7-8 scribbled on it, rephrased for the promises it contained for me:

"Blessed is the mom who trusts in the Lord, whose trust is solely in Him. She will be like a tree planted by nourishment, she doesn't fear when the hot pressure times come, for she will stay cool. She will not be anxious in a drought of strength or time, she will keep bearing the fruit (of the Spirit)."

"Lord, give me strength for this task...to be present with the scrubbing...present with You, and *I trust You* for all the details and messes that my exhausted body just can't rise to tackle tonight."

In that one evening, unlike so many before it, I experienced a victory. Bodies were laid to rest amongst a messy home. But oh, the relief to have walked through the evening entrusting all the details to the power of a God Who promises to show up as we trust in Him! What a relief to treat my family with kindness despite the overwhelm of the spaces needing tending! That night of faith-walking required the humility to be human. And with the humility to be human, I had walked in humility towards my children. The evening ended in peace and rest, not because everything had been accomplished, but because my being and the tasks had been entrusted to my Savior.

When the Circumstances Look Too Bleak

"I will open rivers on the bare heights,

and fountains in the midst of the valleys.

I will make the wilderness a pool of water,

and the dry land springs of water.

I will put in the wilderness the cedar, the

acacia, the myrtle, and the olive.

I will set in the desert the cypress, the plane and the pine together

that they may see and know,

may consider and understand together,

that the hand of the LORD has done this,

the Holy One of Israel has created it."

Isaiah 41:18

During a quiet time, I jotted down my reflections on this passage.

"This passage so perfectly sums up what God does, what He has done, and what He will continue to do. He opens up sources of refreshment and life in places that seem void, lonely, wrong or ugly. He promises rivers, fountains, pools of water, and springs in an environment that seems completely incapable of providing those resources. How can the refreshment of water come in the dry and desolate? Jesus said that He offers the living water that quenches all thirst. He can offer this in any setting, making pools of water in the wilderness of our souls or experiences because He IS the living water. No matter how dire of a wasteland our marriages, our parenting, our finances, or our productivity seems, He can open up rivers there."

While scribbling in my journal, the Lord was fortifying me with truth for when I was to walk through circumstances that would feel too bleak.

I wrote those words while pregnant with our ninth child during the height of the Covid pandemic. As a mom of eight, I had known well the upcoming incredible drain on my energy and body as a new human grew within. My previous 320 months of pregnancy left a mark on the memory. I anticipated desperately trying to keep up with the busy life of managing eight kids, tending to household responsibilities, and ministering alongside my husband, all while in a perpetual state of exhaustion. I also knew from experience, how *worth it* all of it would be as we enjoyed a new human soul entering our family with all of the cuteness, fun and joy they would bring.

I had been wrestling with the Lord about all this, crying out for strength and promises to cling to in the upcoming journey of trust and dependence (just like all the other pregnancies had been).

The reference Isaiah 58:11 had been popping into my mind as I bustled about my day, and I resolved that at the next free moment, I would look it up.

I had stolen a moment away into my room, and there on that needing-to-be-vacuumed carpet, next to that needing-to-be-emptied garbage can, I knelt over my Bible. I read the verse and was undone…

Undone by the ways that Scripture can speak so powerfully, and how the Holy Spirit can pinpoint so clearly the exact promises of God we need for each season of our lives.

> "The Lord will guide you always;
> He will satisfy your needs in a sun-scorched land
> and will strengthen your frame.
> You will be like a well-watered garden,
> like a spring whose waters never fail.'"
> Isaiah 58:11 NIV

I sat in wonder.

The Lord would guide me through this pregnancy.

He would satisfy my needs through this pregnancy.

He would strengthen my tired and overexerted frame during this pregnancy.

And right there, He promised not only to help me survive this pregnancy, but also IN it, I would be a well-watered garden and a spring.

That was enough for me.

The passage was eagerly scribbled on a notecard that would be carried in my purse, recited at the stoplights, and rehearsed when "it all feels too hard."

I could never have imagined just how much I would need these promises the next few months when it "felt too hard" in unexpected ways.

It was the morning of my first ultrasound for this little one and I eagerly bustled around the house to get kids off to school, children set up on zoom school, and toddlers occupied while I would be gone. I was about to turn eleven weeks pregnant and I couldn't believe I was already almost done with my first trimester. Some people had spoken that they thought I would be pregnant with twins, and I eagerly awaited to see if this might be true. As I gave Danny last minute "zoom schooling" instructions, I remember saying, "Twins or not, I just want to see a heartbeat and a healthy baby."

But I never saw a heartbeat.

Instead, as I lay on the bed in the dark ultrasound room, I stared at a screen with a vastly underdeveloped baby on it. And no beautiful throb, throb, throb on the ultrasound screen. The technician "captured" just straight lines going across the monitor.

"There's no heartbeat," I told her.

She curtly told me that the doctor would see me shortly.

I sat in the waiting room and cried. Sniffled behind my mask. Tried not to make a scene. There all alone to sit with my grief – knowing the inevitable but waiting what seemed like an eternity to hear the definite.

I choked through interactions with the rest of the office personnel. Waves of grief and loss and disappointment rushed over me. I left that office sobbing.

Now that I knew the reality that our baby had actually died three weeks prior, it all made sense: The sudden disappearance of nausea. The rush of returned energy I had experienced the week prior. My hair falling out. My lack of a baby bulge that seemed like it should have been growing more by then.

I cried the rest of the day. Distractedly, I tended to children and helped online schoolers with their work. My husband started texting friends and family. I couldn't talk about it; I wanted to retreat into my own little world of grief and sorrow. In the following weeks, I was in a desert, a parched place. The bleak surroundings blurred together.

But streams of water started to well up in that place, just like the Scripture promises that I had clung to early in the pregnancy. I was powerless to move myself *out* of the barren heights, but the trickle of refreshment and sustenance sprung up right there *in* them. Meals were delivered to the house. Cards came in the mail. Stuffed animals for grieving older siblings were dropped off. A hotel reservation was made by a friend so that I could get away to a quiet place to take the medication to kick my body into "labor" in order to pass the baby. Special gifts, and extra spending money, and prayers and love and sympathy flooded in. Jesus, the living water, was welling up right there in the midst of our bleak wilderness, and He was doing it through His people.

"Whoever believes in Me, as Scripture has said, rivers of living water will well up from within them." John 7:38

Well, rivers of water were welling up from within our community and flowing out to refresh me in that place.

Those streams didn't change the surroundings, but they did provide bits of refreshment in the parched place. The desert heat of grief and sorrow and the at-times debilitating heaviness of loss still felt dry and overwhelming. But Jesus was in them. To fight the grief or flee from the sorrow through busyness and numbing would be to actually flee from Jesus.

Jesus, the humble One, was Himself a man of sorrows and acquainted with grief. He, as a man, was not above the whole gamut of human emotion. So I, as His child, could humble myself into the full range of emotion that death brings. To feel all the ache in that place of loss, to feel the sting of pain, and to cry the tears of mourning actually allowed a meeting to occur. It was a meeting with the Savior who had been in that place already and could fellowship with me in the place of suffering and sadness. To put on the "I'm OK" brave face would only emit an aura of false pride and strength. But here I was too undone to muster up the energy for facades. Rather, in the place of weakness, in a humbled place, I found the treasure of fellowship with Jesus and the living water He provides.

The grief never disappeared, but the "cedar, acacia, the myrtle and olive trees had grown up in that space as a testament "that the hand of the Lord has done this," just like Isaiah 48:18 had promised.

When the Circumstances Aren't
What You Want Them to Be

Worry swoops in. As it enters my brain, it swirls and balloons and consumes my thoughts, and therefore my joy. Worry over finances, worry over the state of my children's hearts, worry over my dyslexic kids surviving in school, worry over the thousands of details that come flooding at me all throughout the day. One tried and true indicator of whether humility is pulsing through my life is the level of contentment I am experiencing in any given situation.

Am I focused on the lack?

Am I focused on what I desperately want changed?

Does my mind's eye focus on the yard that needs manicuring, the child whose hardened heart needs changing, the health issues my husband is facing, the marriage that needs growth, the finances that never seem enough?

I want to claw myself out of these uncomfortable scenarios. In a desperate attempt OUT of the unpleasant places, I complain, bark orders at kids, or nag my husband. *What if walking humbly before an almighty God is receiving any set of circumstances with a measure of surrender and gratitude?*

I'll never forget the moment that 1 Peter 5:6 came alive to me in the nitty gritty of my discontentment struggles. I was getting into the car, frustrated by some extra baby weight that felt annoying and uncomfortable. And the words flashed into my mind,

"Humble yourselves, therefore, under the mighty hand of God so that at the proper time He may exalt you."

And the thought came: instead of basing my contentment on the hope of losing the extra weight, what if God's desire for me was to humble myself into the accepting of the extra weight? What if loving Him and loving others even when I hadn't "arrived" in my goals was what He was after? I realized that humbling myself looked like submitting to and even enjoying that season of being somewhat heavier. It was an act of submitting to the mighty hand of God, Whose hand is even over the size of my body. It was in that moment that I realized peace and freedom was mine to enjoy, and the only requirement was humility.

No matter if I deemed a change in my circumstance as the very thing that could make me happy, I was to submit and surrender to the overarching rule of God. No matter what my personal preferences were, I was to receive it all with gratitude because a mighty God ruled over it. Taking circumstances as they are, and believing that this was the exact state in which God wanted my thankfulness, could actually transform my attitude in a single moment. I would find submission and surrender, with gratitude, were the only weapons I had against the multitude of worries that had the potential to swoop me away into a spiral of anxiety.

When I looked up the verse later, I kept reading.

*"Humble yourselves, therefore, under the mighty hand of God so that at the proper time He may exalt you, **casting all your anxieties** on Him, because He cares for you." 1 Peter 5:6*

There it was. The antidote for anxiety again. Right there, I caught a glimpse of the exchange.

Humbling myself under the mighty hand of God could only occur while simultaneously casting my anxieties on Him. I could not both behold the awesome and kind God, revealed through the Bible, while also holding on to the sundry conflicting fears and frustrations that kept me anxious.

The more I relinquished control over all the things, the less anxious I would feel. My mind's death-grip on all the details slowly loosens as I rehearse God's promises. As I speak HIS Word, and His characteristics as laid out in the Scriptures, I come to terms with His abilities. And slowly I choose to thrust the weight of my burdens into His care.

Humbling myself is a declaration of "You've got this, I don't."

And this could happen anywhere and at any point.

If this were the case, humility truly could be the antidote for anxiety.

When the Circumstances Aren't the Real Problem

"Stop your grumbling."

My bleary eyes had just opened on that January morning. Another day to get eight children to all the different places they needed to be no later than 8:00 am and I was tired.

And yet the first thing the Holy Spirit popped into my spirit was, "Stop your grumbling."

I immediately thought about the story of the Israelites who had just been delivered from generations of slavery by God's miraculous provision (Exodus 12). Right after they were miraculously rescued from their captors, they grumbled about food, grumbled about pending danger, complained about water and whined about not having meat. It was so easy to think about "those back then" and how obviously ungrateful they were.

But a complaining spirit had crept in and permeated all of my interactions...complaints about our home, about the messes, about the schedule, about my husband's schedule, about my kids' behavior.

The warning of 1 Corinthians 10 applied not to "them" but to me.

There in that first morning instruction, I received the firm, but ultimately loving rebuke.

"Stop your grumbling."

It was a warning, just like in 1 Corinthians.

"We must not put Christ to the test as some of them did...nor grumble as some of them did and were destroyed by the Destroyer." Now these things happened to them as an example, but they were written down for our instruction,..... Therefore let anyone who thinks that he stands take heed lest he fall." 1 Corinthians 10:9-12

It rolled over in my mind, intermingled with the Scriptures I had read. The Holy Spirit kept speaking into the rebuke, shedding light into the struggle. It was as if He was coaching me through it. His gentle whisperings and rebuke went a little something like this....

"A criticizing tongue is a complaining tongue. When you are so quick to criticize, it's actually a complaint to God for making a person different from the way you, in your inflated self, want them to be.

"Instead of criticizing, allow Me to have room to do the convicting. *How much has your criticism accomplished anyway?* It doesn't bring change, it just drives a wedge between you and your loved one and makes both of you miserable. Instead of trying to help Me accomplish the work I am doing, give Me the space to do MY job."

"Whatever is lovely and pure and of good report and is praiseworthy... think on these things!" Philippians 4:8

"Think on these things in the people around you. Choose to speak about those things into the atmosphere...even if your heart doesn't feel it in the moment."

True faith is hoping in the unseen. True faith is believing that God is making that person around you into a glorious reflection of His Son. True FAITH will hold you back from jumping in and criticizing and correcting and controlling. True faith is TRUSTING in GOD to do His job and not jumping in to try to take it.

I have stumbled in this area a hundred times this week. But today I am believing God will grant the victory to speak life and not death and the grace to hold back and let HIM reign in the other person.

The root of a complaining spirit. Where is it? Why does it come so easily and naturally to me to find something to complain about?

I was pondering these things about myself as I faced yet another day full of mundane tasks that will be undone (and need to be re-done) in the next 24 hours. As my mind wandered, I felt as though I was sinking into the drudgery and even despair of it all.

The Holy Spirit was gentle. He did not condemn and point a finger and say "Look at all I've blessed you with! Why can't you be grate-ful?!?" Instead of condemnation, He showed up with a picture and a strategy.

I saw a picture of a swamp (probably because I myself felt like I was sinking in the muck of the monotony). The swamp wasn't the landscape of my life but rather the landscape of my mind. If I just proceed into my day, allowing my thoughts to drift and land arbitrarily, then inevitably they would land in the mud and quick-sand and start to sink my whole being into despair. Unintentional thoughts would naturally land on the discouraging, the this-needs-to-change, and the frustrating.

The picture of the swamp also had the image of different stones, like stepping stones across it. If I intentionally chose to land my thoughts on the blessings in my life or the precious moments, then it would be like stepping firmly on the solid rocks and I would have a pathway through the swamp. It would take intentionality in my mind to find and step on the blessings in my life, but it would prevent me from landing in the sinking sand of despair. The strat-egy was not to eradicate all potential mud and mire from my view.

The strategy was actually finding the solid spaces of blessing and goodness for my thoughts to land on. The Lord was showing me, once again, the blessed humility of contentment by surrendering to imperfect circumstances touched by the goodness of God.

The picture gave me a whole new view of the Philippians passage,

*"Finally, brothers, whatever is true, whatever is honorable, whatever is just, whatever is pure, whatever is lovely, whatever is commendable, if there is any excellence, if there is anything worthy of praise, **think about these things.**" Philippians 4:8*

It was as if the Lord was inviting me to "land on the stepping stones " by "thinking on these things." It would be the way through. Life is full of drudgery. Whether a mother of many kids or a man in a cubicle working on a computer all day, there are many many non-joy-inducing activities one must engage in. Discouragements, boredom, and frustrations are simply part of living in a world with the curse of sin in it. But because of a good, merciful and loving God, there are always blessings hidden in the muck. These are the stepping stones through the swamp-mercies of God IN our situations rather than mercies of God to rescue us OUT of situations. Humility, or the forsaking of our will for the receiving of HIS almighty will, allows for space to experience joy in the drudgery, and peace in all things.

Seeing and mentally landing on God's goodness in each circumstance allows for Him to be God and for us to simply be objects of His blessings. It is the key for not just enduring the drudgeries of life, but experiencing the joy of His presence in the midst of the drudgeries.

Lord Jesus, I surrender to You my eyesight and my mindsight. You are worthy of it! Right now, I choose to align my mind, my will and my prayers with Your Word. I align my desires with what You have commanded in Philippians 4:8. May I think on what is true and honorable in my children, my husband, and those I interact with today. May I think on what is just and pure. May I see and experience the lovely by having a mind that looks for it. May I see what is commendable in my children, and look at the excellent. May I find what is worthy of praise and talk about it. Because of Jesus's infilling presence, I believe that You can empower me to walk in this reality.

In Jesus' name,

Amen.

Surrounded

"You have hedged me behind and before, And laid Your hand oupn me."
Psalm 139:5 (NKJV)

"You are a hiding place for me; You preserve me from trouble;
You surround me with shouts of deliverance. Selah."
Psalm 32:7

The insurance phone calls need to be made. The two-year-old is whining that the banana has a yucky spot on it. *Are the boys working on their schoolwork? Or do I hear them shuffling Legos around?* I need to run down and switch the laundry to the dryer. A phone call from my daughter at after-school study hall. "Honey, you're going to have to stay at the school until your brother's practice is over. I don't have time to make two trips to the school this afternoon." Click. *Oh! The baby! What is he putting in his mouth?* Finger sweep. Back to that to-do list. *How could I have been going nonstop all day and not ONE thing is moved off that list?!? Ok, where is that insurance card so I can make that phone call?* I call out a panicked "Boys! You better be working on your schoolwork and not getting distracted!" I shut my bedroom door to the sound of nerf guns getting cocked on the other side of the house. I step over the board books strewn all over my floor...and glance at the toilet paper shreds the baby left in the wake of his explorative crawl. I plop down at my desk.

I am surrounded,
All day, surrounded.

But it doesn't feel like the Lord surrounding me, it feels more like assailants.

> *"They surrounded me, surrounded me on every side; in the name of the LORD I cut them off." Psalm 118:11*

I have already had my revelation of God's bigness and goodness, my smallness, and the deliverance from anxiety when we humble ourselves. My mindset is starting to change. But for so long in those moments of feeling so surrounded by needs – children and responsibilities and messes and endless to-do's – I would start to panic. Like a surrounded dog under attack, barking at all who approached, I would bark at my kids: ordering them around, shaming them for their behavior and yelling at them all when I was feeling trapped by the overwhelm. For so long I had thought that "feeling surrounded" could be avoided if I just could get up early and have my quiet time before kids arose, if I could just organize my to-do list better, if I could work harder and fast enough then I could outrun "my pursuers."

It wasn't people that pursued me, it was those tasks and all the needs that threatened to surround, taunt and defeat my desperately-desiring-to-conquer-it-all self.

But the humility to cease and desist, the humility to look up at God's abilities instead of my own, the humility to experience each moment minute-by-minute and task-by-task as one engagement at a time, the humility to trust, could write a different narrative. My pride wants to alter the narrative by conquering the circumstances. Humility provides a different narrative with the same set of circumstances.

Scripture is full of examples of Who and what truly surrounds us, if we have the heart eyes to see.

> "But the LORD's portion is His people,
> He found them in a desert land...
> He surrounded them and watched over them;
> He guarded them... " Deut.32:10 (NLT)

> "You are a hiding place for me; You preserve me from trouble;
> YOU surround me with shouts of deliverance. Selah." Psalm 32:7

> "The angel of the LORD encamps around those
> who fear Him, and delivers them." Psalm 34:7

With humility I can experience peace in the middle of the storm, because there is an eye of the storm. Threats could be swirling all around, but with the presence of Christ, there is a peace that can sustain the human soul no matter what is flooding, swirling or blowing around me. Humility isn't the magic formula for peace in storms; Christ's all-sustaining presence is. Humility is just the heart posture that gets myself out of the way to make enough room for Christ to show Himself to be *there*. His presence is already there, His faithfulness is already true, but it takes a humble posture to be able to slow down enough to see Him working on our behalf.

Ugly pride can keep me very busy doing all the things that seem like serving my family, helping propel my kids' educations and futures, or blessing my community. Pride has no opinion as to what the activity is, whether it seems holy or unholy. It simply wants to keep ME in the seat of authority, running the show, calling the shots. Humility is a posture of the heart and mind, still doing the same things, still in the midst of the same set of circumstances, but it makes room for another to be the sustaining power in it. When I get out of the way, Christ can be the source of righteousness, love, and energy for the service. With His indwelling presence, I can still be busy with all the same activities and ambitions but He can be the power and peace actually accomplishing it.

Accessing this reality is not a once-for-all surrendering of everything. Rather it comes in the moment-by-moment surrendering of myself to the will of the Father. It comes in the task-by-task trust in His almighty capabilities to work through me. It doesn't mean I stop yielding my hands, and feet, and mouth and ears to engage in my full and active life; it means another presence is empowering all those members of my body. Oh, for the grace to surrender! And oh, for the grace to surrender even when I've failed to surrender a thousand times that day! Each new moment is a new opportunity to enter into the humility which leads to surrender, which leads to empowerment.

Father Almighty, I can't change my posture towards You yesterday or today or even moments ago. But right now, in this very moment, I surrender myself to You yet again. I humble myself and my agenda before You so that I can behold more of my God. I will stand by and see the salvation of the Lord which He will accomplish for me today. I trust that You, Lord, will fight for me while I keep silent (Exodus 14:13). I believe You are capable when I am not. I believe that You are the kind and gentle burden bearer when I am not. I believe that I cannot, but I believe You can. Thank You in advance!

In Jesus Name,
Amen.

YOU'RE GETTING ON MY NERVES: HUMILITY IN OUR RELATIONSHIP WITH OTHERS

Start the Day Out Dead

I rise with the alarm because I know how vital these morning times are. I desperately need to renew my mind with the truths of God's Word before the whirlwind of the day begins. I start by jotting down the things I'm grateful for. I read through some Psalms and Proverbs. The words come alive as they connect to the passages in the New Testament that I'm reading. I write out the important things that stick out to me. It is a rich time, and I feel like I have learned so much. The morning starts unfolding and a kid can't find his socks, and a brother hits his sister over the use of the toaster and I forgot a form I was supposed to have filled out and then we're all running late, and the last straw was all the complaining and fighting over who sits where, and I blow it.

I yell at everyone, and the departure to school is a sour one.

And on my drive home, I wonder.

"What happened?!?"

"Lord, I got up and met with You and had this great time of piecing together Scriptural truths, and within 45 minutes all semblance of goodness or godly ambition in mothering went down the drain. What happened???"

And the instructions came.

"Start the day out dead."

That sure sounded encouraging.

But I had been a student of the life of Christ and the power of His indwelling presence long enough to know exactly what He was prompting.

I could have the richest of quiet times, and study in depth the truths and their history and their application. But if it is still ME trying to engage in my day and use the Scriptures to reach my mothering goals, then it is still ME running the show. My old self could not do anything good (Romans 8:3, John 15:5). I could spend the richest of times at His feet trying to gain the wisdom and guidance I needed to embark in my life, and then leave him right there at my quiet time spot! I needed to invite the good Teacher to run the show by showing up not just in the early morning quiet time, but through me, throughout my day.

But first, I had to start the day out dead.

So I started a practice.

I would lie on my face and declare.

"I cannot face or handle this day. If I bring me into the equation it always ends in disaster.

Lord, I give You permission to crucify the old me. May she stay lying here on this carpet. And as I rise, I ask that all of Who You are fill all of who I am. May every person I encounter experience You in me, rather than me in me. Today, may I start this day out dead."

Amazing things would happen after this.

I would show up into situations with this backdrop sense of Jesus showing up through me. I envisioned His heart flowing through me to engage my kids, work on the tasks, or welcome the next visitor into our home. With each overwhelming situation, it was as if I was handing it over to Jesus while simultaneously being the hands and feet that engaged in it. The things that spiraled me into overwhelm, didn't faze me like they normally did. There was a strong confidence that Jesus was showing up in it all.

It wasn't a once-and-for-all exchange though. It was a continual invitation to the King Himself to occupy empty spaces.

Lord, show up here.

A kid crying. *Lord, show up here, flow through me to this child.*

Kids bickering. *Lord, I don't know how to handle this situation, but You do. Show me what to do.*

And this blessed relief would flood me,

"It's not all up to me."

Starting the day out dead takes the pressure off.

And peace, the Prince of Peace, could take up residency.

Free of Yourself

You know what causes the most misery, discomfort and discontent?

It's not my whiny kids or my messy house or rebellious preteens or too many tasks or a husband who has to stay out late for meetings all the time.

It is self.

When I have thoughts of myself and self is the background by which I make my decisions, schedule my time, or treat my family, then anything that shakes the almighty will of self causes me to become undone. If the sovereign reign of self is compromised, then all patience, joy and perspective is lost in any and every circumstance. When the backdrop is self, then, whether I face situations that I feel like I can handle or situations that I can't (like bedtime getting pushed back even further, thus stealing my time to decompress) or offering my home to guests (when I don't feel like I have the extra capacity), then the only empowerment to face the situation is self. With self as the only emotional, physical, or mental resource to offer, I am stunted in every situation, robbed of joy and constantly living in a state of "never enough."

My circumstances don't make me miserable. My prideful self makes me miserable.

What had Murray said about all this? I had read about it in his humility discourse.

The prideful self is ever-hungry for dominance, power, and control. It was the appeal of these objectives that led to that first bite of forbidden fruit which plummeted the entire human race into its fallen state. The appeal to "be like God" is the allure of pride that claims peace, joy and security if only we could reign. If only life could be as we think it ought to be. I doubt Eve was power hungering for rule over the entire cosmos. But to have control over what is here and now and for things to play out as I see fit? This is the lure of every mother, every human. I don't need to rule the nations, I just need to rule "my world." I want to be God over my family, over my home, my body and its appearance, my work, my productivity and even "my ministry." In clamoring for Godlike status in my "world" (albeit a small one), I end up stomping on the people around me – hurting, brushing past, ignoring and even attacking those placed around me to love. It is the enormous chasm between my desire (for control) and my actual ability to be in control that leaves me in a state of limbo, of continual discontent and unrest. I can never truly be in control, so I can never truly be at peace. The words of James ring true,

"What causes fights and quarrels among you (or inside of you?) Don't they come from your desires that battle within you? You want something but don't get it. You kill and covet, but you cannot have what you want." James 4:1-2 NIV

Unless.

Unless I can learn the great antidote provided later in that James chapter.

"Submit yourselves, then to God"(v. 7)

Why?

For the first time after years of reading through the book of James, the correlation washes over me between the conflicting desires and the antidote that submission provides.

Verse 6 says that God gives grace in the circumstance and reminds us of the ancient truth, *"God opposes the proud, but gives grace to the humble."*

The prideful self is the ever-present competitor to the lordship of the only true God. It is the number-one competitor to the trust and surrender that could be ours if we are free from ourselves and our pursuit of godlike status.

Submission to the one true God frees me to rest in the almighty and good sovereignty of God in all circumstances. Freedom and rest are only found in losing sight of myself in view of the majesty and glory of a God who sustains planets in space but also created beauty in the tiniest flower of the common weed. Losing self, rather than finding self, gives grace for trusting in the intricacies and details of life. When I think of the steadfast love of the Lord, instead of thinking of myself – my desires, my comforts, my to-do list and my plans – then I am freed to rest. When I think of the steadfast love of the Lord, then even my failures and shame get lost in the backdrop of how good and in-control God is.

"We have thought on Your steadfast love, O God" Psalm 48:9

The Scissor Miracle

It had been another frantic Sunday morning.

If I had laid the children's clothes out the night before, we wouldn't have had battles over mismatching clothes.

Help me, Lord.

If I had trained my kids better about putting shoes away in their shoe bins, we wouldn't have spent 20 minutes frantically looking under couches and in toy chests for them.

Help me, Lord.

If I had a better chore system, my daughter would automatically do her breakfast chore without mommy asking sixteen times.

Help me, Lord.

If I had gotten up earlier, I would have had Bible time with the kids at the breakfast table instead of barking at them to eat faster so we could leave.

Help me, Lord.

If I were calmer, gentler, maybe there wouldn't be so much bickering and complaining in the car while we drove downtown to church.

Help me, Lord.

If I were a more organized person, my purse wouldn't be so heavy with all the junk that's accumulated in it…in addition to lugging a chunky baby in a car seat carrier.

Help me, Lord.

We're just now rolling into church, and I'm exhausted. The adrenaline rush to get us out the door is starting to crash, and we file into our seats. And all the kids are fidgety. The six-year-old is "hungry again." (We just ate breakfast!) The ten- year- old just took five bagels off the refreshments table on our way into the sanctuary. (I'm telling you, we JUST ate breakfast!) The baby needs a diaper change (I JUST changed it, before we left), and all I want to do is sing some songs to Jesus and not have to deal with anyone else's problem for at least 20 minutes…

Then the whimpering starts…

"Mommy! Mommy! My tag is itching me."

"Honey, I can't do anything about that right now."

"But, moooommmy, it really itches. Can't you cut it off?"

Lord, I know I'm failing miserably at everything…and if I could just get my act together and get more organized, things wouldn't be so hard. But Lord, You're going to have to handle this problem. I give it to You. I have nothing left.

"Mommy, can't you get some scissors and just cut it off…it reeee-aaaalllly iiiiiiiitches…"

"Honey, you're just going to have to deal with it."

We're already halfway through the worship time, and by this time I really need to change the baby's diaper.

I'm fishing through my bag to find a diaper so I can slip out and change it.

And then I feel them.

I had thrown them in there earlier in the week to wrap a gift for someone at stoplights on my way across town because, again, I didn't have my act together, and was wrapping birthday gifts on the fly.

I quickly pulled a pair of miraculous scissors out of my purse and snipped the tag off. Thus relieving me of an entire-worship-service-long whining session.

Thank You, Lord! Thank You!!

I whisper to Him.

And He did some whispering back:

*If you had had your "act" together like you envision and expect for yourself, I couldn't show up in such intimate ways. You wouldn't need **Me**.*

*I take the entirety of your messy life, and **use every part**. Even un-cleaned-out purses and lost shoes and whining children.*

Bring Me itchy tags, and disorganized purses, and frantic mornings, and let Me bear them. I have creative ways of carrying them, while you carry My easy yoke and light burden.

The "extra luggage" that you think is so cumbersome now, might be your answer to prayer later.

Faith as small as a mustard seed...as small as itchy tags, can move mountains. Just watch."

That Sunday morning I learned a lesson that was far more impactful than any sermon I could uninterruptedly listen to. It was a lesson in trusting in a big God Who is in charge of the tiniest of details instead of trusting in the prideful self trying to manage and manipulate all circumstances to be ideal. When my pride falls down and I plunge into the capabilities of the Almighty, I finally experience rest....Even in the midst of crazy morning schedules, and itchy tags.

The Opportunity for Humility with Our Kids

"Do nothing out of selfish ambition or vain conceit.
Rather, in humility value others above yourselves."
Philippians 2:3

I had been wrestling with the behavior of one of my sons. We butted heads at every opportunity possible. It was getting ugly, and tiring, and hopeless. *Am I going to have a lifelong relationship of disgust with him and he with me?* I started asking God to break into a relationship that felt like it was at a total impasse.

In the coming days, a revelation slowly came over me. My attitude towards my child, and the mental tapes I was playing about his heart and his motives led to a certain (and cynical) view of everything he did. I realized what I was thinking was bearing fruit in how I was reacting. Soon a blanketing of what I needed to do came over me as the Holy Spirit exposed my sin, revealed the truth about what was going on and guided me in how to proceed. I needed to retell myself a different narrative about WHO this child was (despite a history of certain behaviors and attitudes). It became so clear as to what the new narrative was supposed to be.

"My son is such a sweet boy. He's searching for love and affirmation. He just wants to be loved and seen."

I began playing this mental tape in the background of my thoughts whenever I thought of him. As I observed his interactions with siblings, even if they were unpleasant ones, I told myself the lines.

"This child is such a sweet boy. He's searching for love and affirmation in his insecurities. He just wants to be loved and seen."

It was not an overnight transformation, but the more frequently I told myself this narrative, the less frequently I jumped to conclusions when I saw unpleasant behavior. The more I replaced *"Ugh, this kid is so rebellious and I don't see how our relationship will ever be mended"* with *"This child is such a sweet kid..."* the more approachable I became, which then allowed for his defensiveness to come down as well.

Andrew Murray says,

"What a solemn thought, that our love to God will be measured by our everyday intercourse with men [or our kids!] and the love it displays; and that our love to God will be found to be a delusion, except that its trust is proved in standing the test of daily life with our fellowmen [or children]." (Murray, p.9)

My love for God and my humility towards Him could be measured and assessed by my attitude towards my children. In my pride, I had declared a final verdict and a judgment of my son based on my prideful but very limited viewpoint of his behavior. For change to occur, It took humility, and a sheepish surrendering of the verdict that my "all-knowing" self had declared for this child. The surrendering of a narrative could only come with a humility to be willing to receive and repeat a new one. The grace to do this was a work of God, because in the months prior I had simply not had the desire or willingness to see things in any other light.

Pride. It doesn't budge. It isn't teachable. It sees no fault in itself. Humility, on the other hand, is a dependence on a living God Who is actually speaking to us, redirecting us and sometimes rebuking us. It is only with His presence empowering us that we can live out humility towards those around us.

The funny thing about parenting eight children is that as soon as you get through one crisis season with one child, another crisis pops up with a different one (God is merciful that they don't all happen at once usually). So there I found myself several months after having enjoyed the benefits of a more tender relationship with my once-hardened son, and similar issues started popping up with my daughter. Somehow every interaction was turning into a fight. Somehow disagreements over basic chores and household responsibilities turned into war zones. Our entire relationship consisted in explosive interactions about responsibilities and the subsequent dislike of the other. Then there was my self-loathing for not being able to strategically handle these issues better.

I started praying into the same type of "answer" God had given me with the other child. Except instead of a strong sense of a new narrative to be telling myself about the situation, there was silence. I couldn't "write" a new narrative in my head. Nothing would stick. I couldn't sense what I needed to be believing about her. After a few weeks into the prayer wrestlings, finally I got some clarity. A gentle voice said,

"Let ME be her God."

This new directive was different than the previous one. This required more a posture of the heart than a proactive telling of a narrative. Instead of a mantra to be recited, there was space to be given. But space couldn't be given unless trust was being worked out. This trust had to have confidence in an almighty, good and all-encompassing God who could convict, speak to, and work in my daughter without me charging into that space in order to do the correcting, rebuking, and criticizing. Once again, humility (the viewing of God more than self) and trust (the confidence in His abilities rather than my own) were the only remedy for the pride-propelled parenting. The only thing I accomplished when I tried to charge into the situation and bring about my will was collateral damage to my kids and to my relationship with them. Only God could bring about the character growth and peace I desired to see in our relationship. Murray says it this way,

"Humility means the giving up of self and the taking of the place of perfect nothingness before God. (Ch. 10, pg 32) This is the nothingness that makes room for God to prove His power." (Ch. 6, pg 21)

Let me tell you. This type of humility is SO hard. It is like a foreign invader to our natural inclinations. It truly feels impossible in the grind of large family life, logistics, wide ranges of ages, emotions, needs and requirements. *Pure conformity to Almighty Mother's WIll" would make things run a lot more easily and efficiently, wouldn't it? But the humility to always take into consideration the "other"? The humility to lay down the Omniscient Task List" in order to go slow enough to allow God to have the time and space to work in our children rather than US work in our children?* Indeed, it seems as mighty a task as moving a tombstone on the

MEMOIR FROM THE MANIC YEARS

third day, or thrusting the mountain into the heart of the sea. But there is hope. There is hope for us to live into it and hope for our children to grow up under it.

Humility gives a different way of interacting with others, and a different way of viewing those frustrating behaviors in our children and others. This freeing viewpoint can only be obtained while treasuring Christ and the humility in which He, Himself, walked. Murray calls out those who want to do big things for Christ but have yet to realize that the real sacrifice and surrender that Christ calls us to is actually manifested in how we treat and react to those who are getting on our nerves. A modern paraphrase of Murray's conclusion to his chapter entitled "Humility in Daily Life" reads,

"And why is it that men [and moms] who have joyfully given up themselves for Christ find it so hard to give up themselves for [their children and] the trying people in their lives? Is not the blame in the ways modern Christianity is trumpeted? Realize your dream! Fulfill your destiny! Make way for you. The Church has so little taught that the humility of Christ is actually the first of virtues to be pursued. Humility is the truest power that comes from the Holy Spirit. To walk in the 'power of the Holy Spirit,' humility is the very posture needed in order for that power to manifest."

Murray continues,

"If this virtue has been forgotten in your daily life and Christian walk, do not be discouraged. Let the discovery of the lack of this grace stir us to greater expectation from God. Let us look upon every child, situation or individual who

tries us, vexes us or just plain gets on our nerves, as God's means of grace. Their very annoyance to us is actually God's instrument for our purification and an opportunity for the humility of Jesus to be breathed into us and manifested through us. Let us have such a faith in the All Encompassing Fullness of God and also the nothingness of self, that we move forward to love and serve others, including our children, with complete abandon to His power and priority and not our own." (Ch 6, pg 22)

A Practical Way to Get Lower.. with Your Voice

I'd given up trying to have my quiet time in the house. It was as if a radar went off in my small children when I awoke. I would ever-so-quietly get myself situated with my journal and Bible and prayer lists. Approximately three minutes after having just gotten situated, someone (or many someones) would suddenly need to use the bathroom, need a blanket, need to cuddle with me (aka lie on my journal) or need to play next to me (which most often just resulted in ripped Bible pages; they make such a great crinkling noise!).

So there I was walking up and down the street in front of my house and reading my Bible.

The idea had come to me as I lamented to God about the pointlessness of getting up to meet with Him if I was just going to have to be in kid-maintenance mode. I had even recruited prayer partners to pray that I would be able to get that vital alone time to read Scripture, think, and pray. It struck me one morning at

6:23 am: an idea that I never would have thought of on my own, a creative solution that the Holy Spirit birthed in my mind. (That's usually how it is when He is speaking to me.)

"Go outside and walk and read."

So I did.

I grabbed my little travel Bible and went outside and started walking back and forth on my street. Still within earshot of a beckoning child on the porch, I could "hide" down the street but still be available.

I started praying and meditating on the humility verses I had scribbled on those (now) tattered index cards so that I could easily tote them with me in the car, or by the kitchen sink, or now in hand during my "walking quiet time." These were verses that I knew were inroads to the joy, freedom, and release that I had experienced when first realizing the value of humility in my daily life.

> *"Humble yourself under God's Mighty hand so*
> *that in due time He may lift you up."*
> *1 Peter 5:6*

> *"...you SET your heart to understand and humble*
> *yourself before your God..so your words have been*
> *heard and I have come because of your words."*
> *Daniel 10:12*

> *"Whoever exalts himself will be humbled, and whoever*
> *humbles himself will be exalted." Matthew 23:12*

"Whoever humbles himself like this child is the greatest in the kingdom of heaven."
Matthew 18:4

As I walked, I pondered how to practically live this out in the hustle and bustle of my daily life. Yes, there were times that I could physically get on my face and seek to humble myself in mind, spirit and body before God, but what about all the times there are eight kids needing me and I don't have the "luxury" of doing so? Quiet moments are few and far between during the middle of the motherhood years, but there had to be a way to consistently be engaging in a physical act of humbling myself.

Then it washed over me, the still small voice and the practical "answer"...

"Every time you humble your tone of voice before your children, you are humbling yourself before ME."

It was as if Jesus had spoken it to me. It was the wisdom I was asking for, like what James 1 says. I can ask for and expect to receive wisdom and direction from a generous God Who delights to give it. (James 1:5-7)

"If any of you lacks wisdom, let him ask God, who gives generously to all without reproach, and it will be given to him."

God had given me very tangible action I could do in the next fifteen minutes of my life in order to humble myself before the Lord.

"For just fifteen minutes, control nothing but the tone of your voice...a gentle whisper. Meek and gentle. Let your gentleness be evident to all. Go, walk humbly before your God." (Micah 6:8)

I might not be able to go lay prostrate in my closet as often as my prideful heart needed, but the way I could actively "prostrate" myself before the Lord was in the actual tone of my voice. God was giving me so many opportunities to physically humble myself through the natural events of my day- in the tiny moments with my children by looking them in the eye, or stopping what I'm doing to give full attention or through gently talking to them. When I did these things as a means to encountering my Savior, they weren't forced behavior modification to do my mothering job well. They were acts of expectation to meet the living Lord Jesus in them.

Marriage and a Game of Hide-and-Seek

One July, I found myself writing a letter to a friend a week before she was to be married:

As you move into marriage, may you never forget Who ultimately has led you into it, Who delights in the flourishing of it, and Who is the Covenant Keeper Who will sustain you through it. Greater love has no one than this, to lay down your life for your friend. (John 15:13) How perfectly God has designed [your husband] for you and you for [your husband]. What a sweet friendship God has brought about throughout the years, and it will be a joy to lay down your life in the tiny choices of life in order to see him flourish and live. And do you know what is the greater reward than even seeing him flourish or seeing your marriage thrive? It's this intimacy you gain with Jesus when you join Him in the hidden acts of service. Jesus died to His will, yielded to the Father's will, and then proceeded to the cross and to the dark, hidden tomb. Every time you willingly give up your will, yield to the Father's by yielding to your husband's, then you are taking up a cross and following on Jesus' path. On that path, you meet Him. Philippians 3:10 talks about knowing Jesus. The best way to really get to know Him is getting to join Him in the fellowship of suffering. That suffering might be the smallest of hidden choices to serve and surrender. With the suffering comes a knowing and a joining in the power of the resurrection. It is rarely in the BIG sacrifices that Christ will call you, but actually in the small, tiny, seemingly-insignificant ones. But if you follow your Savior in this path of crosses that lead to resurrections, the reward of His Presence and fellowship is the sweetest it can be. That sweetness will cause you to enjoy your new husband and this marriage all the more. After little deaths, you come out on the other side with greater resurrection joy, life and power.'

The funny thing is, I really needed to be writing it to myself – sixteen years, and eight and a half kids into my own marriage.

My husband had been working so hard, and then had gotten quite ill. I had been solo parenting eight children, during the most intense time: back-to-school season. Getting eight children ready to go back to different schools is a very daunting job. During the frenzy of activities, I hardly tended to my spouse. He technically could have stopped breathing down there in that guest room (when you have this many kids, you hide away in random rooms in order to recover), but I wouldn't have found out until the evenings when I finally got a chance to go down and check on him.

But yet, my selfish heart was caught up with all the burdens that I was bearing. The burden of parenting. The burden of a thousand and one details and logistics. The burden of all the driving back and forth to sports practices, and orientations and school shopping. I was slightly annoyed. I almost felt like he "owed" me because of all that I was shouldering alone. And the poor man was down there fighting off aches and chills and headaches and delirium.

I'm so glad I was forced to write that marriage message. This amnesiac forgets that DEATH is actually to be DESIRED. I had started to forget all that I had learned, and all that I had gained through Murray's humility book!

In the losing of self, or the taking up of ones' cross, one gets to practice humility. In the service of others one "enters in" to a place, a hiding away in the tomb of one's own desires or will. In that hiding spot, one finds a Savior Who hid away in the shelter of absolute obedience and surrender to the Father. Yes, death was involved. It wasn't a pleasant process, but the resurrection on the other side not only brought Jesus glory but brought an expanded family. There is fullness that God delights to bring about when we are willing to LOSE ourselves. When we hide away in loss of self, we play a game of hide-and-seek. We hide away in the Father's will, no matter how humble, mundane, hidden and unnoticed it is...and it is that place that Jesus Who seeks and saves the lost, FINDS us, and we Him.

May I never shirk from the hiding.

Instead of hiding *from* the Father (and fear of His will), I will hide IN the Father, and trust His good will.

Great things await us as we play this game of hide-and-seek. And how much more so when we do it with our spouse, who is to be flesh of our flesh and bone of our bone, a relationship which mirrors Jesus, the bridegroom and we, His purified bride.

So sleep on, honey. Get better. And I will find Jesus in the midst of shouldering burdens and responsibilities too big for me. I have a very sufficient Savior Who will find me as I play this game of hide-and-seek.

chapter 7

THE INNER CRITIC; HUMILITY IN OUR SELF-TALK

What Will Be Remembered

Which moment will they remember? I wondered.

It was my few moments of quiet after the morning rush of home-school lessons and household chores and just before the "storm" of the afternoon of loading five kids up to pick up the other three who would inevitably have school drama woes, homework head-aches, and papers to sort through. All this in addition to the fact that I would have dinner to make, mouths to feed, a kitchen explosion to clean up and the bedtime routine that strongly resembled the herding of cats.

But right now, I had one hour for the little kids to nap and have quiet reading time. One hour to try to calm down, collect my thoughts and emotions, and get refreshed enough to plunge back into it all. One hour before I would be moving 100 miles per hour in engagement with eight small people who all had a will and agenda of their own, which often stood in contradiction to my agenda to "get it all done."

So here in the quiet moment, I pondered,

What will they remember?

Will they remember the extra stories I read to the whole crew who slowly but surely stopped what they were doing to come listen as I read to the baby and the two-year-old? Even my tough-kid nine-year-old had huddled over my shoulder as I read the rhymes, recounted the fables, and rolled over words that took us into other worlds. Will they remember the extra time spent to savor that moment, even though it was cutting into "my" down time after a bustling morning? Will they remember the sweet moment that came at the expense of "my" only moments to myself until the last of the teen kids finally went to bed later tonight?

Or will they remember the frustrated outburst twenty minutes into quiet time (after we had finished our endearing reading time) when children were still emerging from their rooms, still loudly chattering, and still keeping the toddlers from their all-important-to-my-sanity-(and theirs!)-nap?

"If I hear your voices one more time, I'm gonna pop your mouth!"

The ugly threat slid over my tongue just as fast and easily as the Dr. Suess rhymes I had been reading just moments before.

I defeatedly slumped back into my bedroom. Reaching past the stack of mail that still needed sorting, I plopped my Bible open. There on that first page, God spoke truth to me in the midst of the defeat over my frequent failings.

"I am He ho blots out your transgression for My own sake, and I will not remember your sins." Isaiah 43:25

I pondered it. So many times, so many years I would sink into mom-fail mode and slink through the rest of the day wearing the shame of my frequent failures to be loving and kind. The shame never helped. If anything, it propelled the frustration and irritability as I fought an inner battle of self-defeat.

He blots them out.

I blot up my kids' spills with a paper towel. The towel absorbs it all, and then I have a clean fresh space on the counter to work. The paper towel gets thrown out. The mess is gone. I had done it and watched it happen a thousand times. I realized I had a decision to make right here. *Would I accept this blotting out? Truly live like all my failures were soaked up and removed like those Bounty paper towels absorb spilled milk? Accept God's Word over my own standards in this moment?*

I had a choice here. My pride wanted to value my performance and my ability to "be a good mom" (that ability was highly lacking). My pride wanted to self-punish if I could not fulfill my self-imposed standards. I could continue to put my confidence in myself, and allow my joy and contentment to rise and fall based on my abilities. I could wallow in mom-guilt or I could rev up my penitence act with renewed resolve to be kind and patient with my children. I could look up mom-anger podcasts to give me more tips about keeping my cool when things weren't going my way.

Or.

I am He Who blots out your transgression.

I could believe this. I could choose to believe what God says, instead of what I say about myself. I could forsake what I could see (the circumstances in which I "fail") and instead grab hold of what I could not see (the promises of a new reality). Hoping in the unseen, and truly believing God's Word over me required...humility. I used to think that ruminating over how awful I was could be counted as humility. But I was beginning to realize that it takes NOT looking at self at all, but rather gazing on the completeness of God's sacrifice for me, that allowed for the humility-induced freedom to infiltrate my life. It is self-righteous pride that wants to hope in *my* performance, *my* resolve, *my* efforts, even *my* feelings about myself. In a place of humility, it becomes easier to simply believe and trust the Word of God over what I'm thinking or feeling. It is choosing Him over me, His declarations over my own.

"I am He who blots out your transgression for My own sake, and I will remember your sins no more." Isaiah 43:25

This Word could make me free right now, right here, right in the middle of my failures.

If I would simply lay down such a big view of myself, and take up the Word spoken over me in Christ as the BIGGER narrative, then I could walk in freedom and release. I could walk in being forgiven. I could experience full availability to God, my children and even myself all by simply believing what this ancient Script said to be true.

"I will forgive their wickedness and will remember their sins no more." Hebrews 8:12

It was almost laughable as this epiphany washed over me. Who on earth do I think I am, if I think I need to hold on to and remember my sins when the God of the universe has already declared that *He* remembers them no more? Who on earth do I think I am, if Jesus, the pure, spotless, Holy One absorbed the weight of my selfishness, pride and harsh words, and I fail to live like He did? Is my own action more important than this one epic climax of all Old Testament prophecies of redemption and healing?

That's pride right there, sistah, masking itself as penitence.

And God opposes the proud.

I remembered hearing (in my incessant audiobook replaying while doing daily dishes) the words of Andrew Murray.

"Humility is often identified with penitence and contrition. As a consequence, there appears to be no way of fostering humility but by keeping the soul occupied with its sin. ... [but humility is usually mentioned in the Scriptures] without any reference to sin...It is simply the displacement of self by the enthronement of God. Where God is all, self is nothing" (Ch 8, p. 26)

It takes a humbling, and a loss of self and self-effort, to accept the Gospel. Right now, right here, the only way to move forward in humility, move closer to Jesus, would be to apologize to my children and let myself go free, because God said I was, whether I think I deserve it or not.

I walk out of my room, knowing those abuses I threatened hung on the tree with the abuses Jesus endured, and I walk into those kids' rooms, and confess that I was mean to say those things that way. I could pray and believe, "God, dwell here, in me. Use me, here in this home, just as I am, in all my stumbling mess".

And He would.

You better believe we had a far better afternoon than if I had spent hours listening to anger management podcasts.

And hopefully, that will be what was remembered.

God's Goodness Leap

My heart stopped. I had to fight to catch my breath. But this wasn't the breathlessness that came with the panic attacks of postpartum anxiety. This was the breath-catching of wonder. Of awe. Of *"Could this really be?"*

A vision came to the forefront of my mind. It was as if I was on the brink of a high precipice, gazing on a magnificent view. If I took the leap, I would plunge myself out into the wind, soaring in the wide open expanse of exhilaration, in complete freedom, but also completely out of control.

I was having an epiphany, a breathtaking epiphany. I had not been in concentrated prayer or in a state of fasting or even listening to a sermon. No, I was shuffling laundry around, making beds, scrubbing burnt oatmeal from the pot and sweeping fifty percent of the breakfast I had just served off of the floor. (How this manages to happen every meal time, I do not know!) I was in the middle of doing all these mundane tasks, the cyclical ones I do daily, but it was as if someone had opened a window and a cool spring breeze had blown in. Except it had blown into the window of my mind...and my heart had skipped a beat. *Is this how Mary had felt when her very mundane day had been interrupted by the angel's announcement that the Christ Child would be interrupting all of humanity's broken history? Could I be experiencing this kind of miraculous disturbance into my day?* For me, it felt like it.

The breathlessness again. The heart thrill of a crazy adventure before me. The adrenaline of the new, and unknown, and excitement and anticipation.

What if....what if...no, it seemed too good to be true.

God's goodness would be too extravagant, too generous, too abundant and far too unearned.

Yes, I was on a cliff, coming to a point of decision. The mountain I stood on was the mountain of what *I* could do. I clung to it. The control felt safer. It was the solid rock of *trying* to be close to God, *trying* to have joy, *trying* to be a patient mother, *trying...always trying.* It was a far cry from the freedom and soaring I read of in Isaiah 40:31

"But those who hope in the Lord will renew their strength.
They will SOAR on wings like eagles;
They will run and not grow weary,
They will walk and not grow faint."

Here I was, with an invitation to leap and plunge into the soaring. I had come to the end of what I could accomplish or climb. I had labored up this mountain, forcing myself forward through duty in the drudgery, disciplining myself to offer thanks, showing up daily to study the promises of God and daily starting my day on my face in a place of reverent humility.

I had done all that I knew to do to grow closer...to ascend the mount of God. Indeed, God had strengthened me to this point, but maybe He was inviting me into a more radical reliance, and with it, a more radical freedom.

This was the epiphany: God Almighty was inviting me to *actually receive* His abundant goodness and His extravagant love. No strings attached. To view all things through the lens of His goodness. To see every gust of wind as Him being a good God to His beloved daughter.

This invitation contradicted every natural impulse to always contribute, earn, achieve, do.

To truly fly – to know the peace and the light burden and the exhilaration of another force completely carrying you would require a jump off of every stable thing I had known. This journey on the road of humility was now leading me to a place of absolute trust. God was inviting me to leave my dependence on my works and fling myself into the expanse of HIS character. *Could I really float on the wind of His grace, His goodness?*

This would require an entirely new mindset. The invitation looked so thrilling, but my track record was so daunting. If Jesus is making all things new (Revelation 21:5), could He make my mindset, my very way of functioning, *NEW*?

We often frame our current experiences in light of our early formative years. Up to this point, I had been functioning in the hard work habits that I had learned as a young person. At the age of 13, when I had just begun budding in my relationship with Christ and my own personal communion with Him, my world began to unravel. My mom mysteriously changed from a vibrant woman committed to serving those around her, to a woman who stayed at home and read the same newspaper over and over again. Months later came the diagnosis of a malignant brain tumor pressing on the part of her brain controlling her personality and drive. Then came the surgeries. The chemo. The radiation. The trips to the hospital. The hair falling out. The home rhythm unraveling, and I, as the oldest daughter, taking on the burden to fight for some sort of normalcy. Then there was a move across states, as my father lost his job and took a new one. Then finally, my beloved mother's death after having battled for two grueling years all that cancer brings. What followed was the onset of deep grief, depression, confusion, and even suicidal thoughts.

I learned in those early teen years that life was hard and burdensome. God was faithful, but life was hard. In the crisis of slowly losing my mother, God had met me in powerful ways to sustain me. I learned that Jesus would meet me in grief and sorrow. In the storm, I grew to know my Savior's intimacy. But long after that season had passed, I continued to function in crisis, almost in an attempt to not lose the God I had grown to love in the midst of this early life trauma. *Was I willing to know Him in a different way? Could I still have intimate fellowship with Him as His Hebrew name Toviya, good God, and not only "God of all comfort"? (1 Corinthians 1:3)*

In this moment, He was inviting me to meet Him in JOY: in laughter and lightness and freedom. I had not known such things as a young teen, so I began to view all unplanned things as struggle and hardship, just as the unplanned cancer diagnosis had been. Having a lot of kids – this was a crisis. Having our family in full time ministry-this – was a crisis. Inviting struggling, under-resourced families and individuals into our lives – this led to crisis. It was like I wanted to view all things in life as a crisis, just in order to stay connected to God. *But what if He was inviting me to connect with Him in complete trust and joy and freedom? To live life in the reality of God completely carrying me? It seemed far too freeing, too wonderful, too easy.*

To live a life in complete joy and surrender to God's goodness and favor would take some mind shifts. There would be nothing new or different about my life. But maybe those same exact settings could be a place where I see and experience the Lord's abundant goodness. If I truly stepped out in faith off the cliff but out into the wide open sky, I could be contentedly joyful in any and every circumstance, because I knew that God was working ALL things for my good, just like Romans 8:28 tells me.

"And we know that for those who love God all things work together for good, for those who are called according to His purpose."

This beckoning into JOY was actually a beckoning into humility.

I was being invited into a humbling of my own ideas on how I thought my life should go. A humbling of my own priorities, so that the joy of relationships could flood in. A humbling of those mindsets and viewpoints that often set *me* up as the judge and jury of the people and circumstances around me. I was being invited to trade them for hope in a mighty God who promised to be working all things together for good.

He was inviting me to take the plunge. "I AM GOOD." Period. No questions asked. His goodness had already been proven with the gift of His own Son, proven with the very blood of Jesus. His own Son sacrificed Himself and bore the burden of my sin, and the burden of all things broken, including every crisis I could ever face or struggle through. He did it to make me an object of the Father's goodness, a recipient of the good gifts that God the Father bestows. (James 1:17)

The actual stepping out "into thin air" would come through believing it to be so, simply taking God at His Word. It would come by faith, not by sight. No matter what. In the tiniest moments in the most mundane circumstances. If I truly thrust myself into the expanse of God's faithfulness, compassion and goodness, I would start to soar. I could start flying into His character with just the wings of faith. I could start praising God and "giving thanks in all circumstances" (1Thessalonians 5:18) truly from my heart. Then

I could freely start doing what I had dutifully forced myself to do in the past.

In the praising, I would practice tangible acts to help move my heart to be TRUSTING that His goodness was prevailing over every situation.

Reciting the Life Lessons

"You are good. You are good."

I told it to myself as I loaded kids into the car, buckled all four car seats and tried to leave the driveway with my zoomschooling child trying to log in on my hotspot. (Gotta love the COVID years!) I left my phone in the house. *Ugh. I would be late AGAIN. Boys would be logged off of zoom class AGAIN. I would have to face my inability to keep all the parts of my life moving AGAIN.* I ran into the house, allowing all the smudges on our dirty front door to irk me. I grabbed my phone, went to start the car, and it wouldn't make a sound. Mind racing to plan B, I ran to fetch the keys of my husband's clunker work truck.

I slammed up against that same smudgy door as I sprinted back into the house. "You are good. What You do is good. Humbling is good." As I swung the dirty door open, the thought hit me. *If I would be living in this thrilling plunge into the goodness of God, it would take an act of belief, in all the tiny, grating, gritty things of life. This life of trust is not some broad-stroked idea. It would take an act of choosing to flap wings on the thin air of frustrating circumstances and stressful situations. It would take choosing to thrust the eyes of my heart onto the goodness of God instead of the emptiness of the conditions around me. There would be no flying without the positioning of my thoughts on HIM Who causes me to soar instead of the positioning of thoughts on my own ability to navigate the stresses of this life as they come hurtling at me.*

I move all the car seats into the smelly cramped space of my husband's work truck. I listen to my boys squabbling about seats. And I insert into the tension of the situation:

"Thank You, Lord, for Your goodness."

"Thank You for the miracle of having the key to this clunkety old truck at the house (and not on my husband's key chain)."

"Thank You for the strength and energy to move all these car seats."

My mind recites "my lessons" back to me. I need it for this pop quiz.

"There is a reason that our twelve-passenger van needs to sit in our driveway today. God is good. There is a reason that the truck key happened to be hanging on the hook today. God is good. There is a reason I am pulling into this carpool line with a busted up truck with a dented door that won't shut right. God is good. Thank You for this opportunity to be humbled by the car I was driving, humbled by the tardiness of my arrival, and humbled by the embarrassment of having to cram this many little humans into the cab of the truck. God, You are good."

God ordained these scenarios. The humbling ones. The ones that put on display to myself and to others the fact that I can control nothing. The ragged cliff of my own doing will only keep me stuck.

But with those humbling scenarios, He beckons me into the flight of faith. Because of this, I can be so thankful for them. Even welcome them. I have no other choice but to audaciously fling myself out in the wide open of soaring on the promises of God's goodness alone.

He's teaching me how to fly.

Because He is good.

Even When You Forget

I'm seated in a newly renovated, spacious house, and I just finished typing the above entry, transferring it from scribbles in my tattered composition notebook to a book format on my computer.

I am in awe.

I had completely forgotten about that entry, forgotten about the visual of jumping into God's goodness and soaring on wings like eagles. Forgotten about the breathtaking moment when God invited me into it.

But the events of this past year have actualized that picture.

For the duration of this past year I have been praying for a new home for our family-of-ten-crammed-into-a-1950s-bungalow. In situations in the past, I have prayed for such specific things like microwaves or flooring or paint or furniture when the needs have arisen. As I began praying for a new home (so our ministry partner and his family could buy ours and move into the neighborhood), I did not feel impressed to pray about the details of our new home. No, as I was on a prayer walk one day, I sensed an invitation, "Pray My character of goodness of the home I might provide for you."

So I went and looked up verses in the Bible about God's character of goodness. I scribbled them out on index cards. Those index cards became my tattered friends. They were alongside with me at all times, so I could proclaim and pray those promises out loud in carpool lines, on runs, in-between-sports-practices, while on morning prayer walks.

"You are good, and what You do is good; teach me Your decrees." Psalm 119:68

"Every good gift and every perfect gift is from above, and comes down from the Father of lights, with Whom there is no variation or shadow of turning." James 1:17

"I would have lost heart, unless I had believed that I would see the goodness of the Lord in the land of the living." Psalm 27:13

"On the glorious splendor of Your majesty, and on Your wondrous works, I will meditate. They shall speak of the might of Your awesome deeds, and I will declare yYur greatness. They shall pour forth the fame of Your abundant goodness and shall sing aloud of Your righteousness." Psalm 145:5-7

"If you then, being evil, know how to give good gifts to your children, how much more will your Father Who is in heaven give good things to those who ask Him! " Matthew 7:11

"Oh, taste and see that the Lord is good; blessed is the man who trusts in Him! " Psalm 34:8

"Oh, that men would give thanks to the Lord for His goodness, and for His wonderful works to the children of men! For He satisfies the longing soul, and fills the hungry soul with goodness." Psalm 107:8-9

"The Lord is good, a stronghold in the day of trouble; and He knows those who trust in Him." Nahum 1:7

For nearly a year, I prayed those prayer verses, and stalked real estate apps desperately trying to find a property that could house our large family. All to no avail.

And then there was the night that I, on a whim, took a pregnancy test after everyone was asleep. Those two lines popped up, and the wrestling began. It was a wrestling match like that of Jacob. I've never spent an entire night awake, praying, praising, crying and studying. But this night I did. Those two lines meant another major shift for our family, another nine months of complete exhaustion, another nine months of putting my budding ambitions on hold for the sake of "just barely surviving", another nine months of forcing my body to keep up with the demands of eight children plus a full life of incarnational urban ministry. All this in addition to the question, *"WHERE will we put another human being in this little house?"* In addition to the dread of what my body and mind would endure the next several months, I was utterly helpless and incapable of moving our family forward into a bigger property.

A few weeks later, my husband and I were on a date night, and went on a prayer walk. We were both feeling restless, like there were endeavors and missions that we were supposed to begin, but not knowing what they were. While we played a worship song, I got a picture so vivid.

I was on a cliff ledge. My back was up against the rock wall behind me and I was desperately trying to stay there. My feet were being inched forward, begrudgingly, towards the edge of the cliff. It was as if the Lord spoke into the situation. "Will you willingly run and leap and soar off this cliff? Or will you have to be dragged off of it? Either way, you are meant to soar, so you can willingly, joyfully thrust yourself into it, or you can make it difficult and tedious."

An hour later, we on a whim decided to look up houses in Stone Mountain, GA where Danny has been serving as a temporary (or so I thought) interim pastor of a small, diverse Presbyterian church. Every time we were up in the urban poverty-moving-in-to-forsaken-suburbs area I had said in my heart, *"Oh, Lord, just please don't call us to a place like this."* Despite zero desires to move there, out of curiosity we just wanted to see what types of houses were available in our price range.

Well, we randomly texted our realtor friend that night when we found a house we were interested in. He immediately got us on the phone with a lender, who at 11:39 pm was taking us through the pre-approval process. The next afternoon we walked into a house that I could immediately "see" my children running through, and "see" renovations that would allow for hospitality and house church, and "see" how the space was almost perfectly pre-designed for all that we desired a home to be...both for our family of 10 and all those we wished to serve. The only problem was that it was in that exact area that I had begged God NOT to send us to.

My head was spinning. Twenty-four hours earlier, I had no intention of ever uprooting our family from our church, our ministry, our schools, our friendships, and our neighborhood. *Could God's goodness leap invitation mean running wholeheartedly into this opportunity for our family to start something new while living on the other side of the city? Could my begrudging feet be holding onto what "was" instead of what could be?* To do something so insane would have needed a "vision" beforehand, because there is no way my logical mind could have wrapped around this outlandish proposition.

The following weeks brought confirmation that this home that I had been praying for over a year, was now manifesting and quickly being given to us. It was just in the "wrong place." The kind owner accepted a lowball bid on a house that was already reduced in price. The owner allowed us to come see it multiple times despite the fact our three-year-old took a bite out of every single one of the plums he had on the counter while we were busily talking about roofs and tree removals. A friend recommended a Christian school that could serve our wide range of ages plus our dyslexic children...just fifteen minutes from the new house. Then there was the collection of believers asking for the structure of collaborative impact among house churches in the area (what we had already been doing in inner city Atlanta). Even a preacher in a church service STOPPED his sermon to interject "There is someone here worrying about a house, and the Lord is saying, 'Don't be anxious. This process is going to be seamless. Don't worry, I have gone before you in this."

Here I was experiencing it. I was running and leaping into the thrill of this adventure and it was exhilarating to see His wild wind surround and uphold me. I was living a picture and a vision that God had given me not once but twice! His goodness was being put on display. As I let go of my control and as I let Him be God, I could soar.

There would be many more opportunities to stand on the promise of His goodness, invitations into blind trust, forcing my mind to be at rest in His presence as the thousands of details of renovating a house, time constraints, packing, and juggling kids and their hearts through the transition. All the stressful details could have threatened to engulf the joy of the manifestation of God's promises, but oh, the thrill of it all! When you have to move in and don't have a working kitchen sink or a washer and dryer for three weeks, the trusting in His goodness is more of an intentional choosing rather than a free-for-all flight. The wind of God's abundance, His compassion, and His fullness surrounded us, but some flapping the wings of faith were required in the soaring. His invitation to leap off the cliff led me to experience and do the very thing I had prayed for all those many months:

"[I] will speak of the might of your awesome deeds, and I will declare Your greatness. They shall pour forth the fame of Your abundant goodness." Psalm 145:6-7

CONCLUSION

I was packing a suitcase at 4:00 am. The night before I had dozed off to sleep-a nursing baby daughter at my side, a half-packed bag on the floor and a pile of clean laundry waiting to be folded-all before I was about to leave my family for a full five days. I was scheduled to travel up to New England for a family wedding, so my husband decided to send me early for the sake of the cheaper flights. As my 40th birthday present, he was giving me a writing week to allow me time to finish this very book while staying with our retired friends in Boston. It was high time the manuscript was completed and sent to editors. I had grown and given birth to yet another baby, after experiencing the painful miscarriage mentioned earlier. It had been three years since first starting the humility memoir on the now crumpled pages of the worn composition book. I had walked through yet another season of postpartum anxiety after that new (ninth) baby. Now I was editing and relearning the truths of what I had written previously as a prescription for the anxious soul.

Scuttling about my closet, fear and anxiety sucker-punched me, reached into the core of my being and began twisting and turning every aspect of who I was.

"What kind of mother actually leaves her entire family to go writing? You aren't even a professional writer. Who do you think you are? How can you leave all the millions of moving parts to go do this? Maybe this isn't God's will. You should back out. Right now. Purposefully miss your flight. Call your hosts and tell them you can't come."

In the dark, the towering stack of clothing toppled as I scurried to fold and put away while my husband caught a few more moments of sleep. I don't think I could handle the agony of being in one place (Boston) while so many people and details needed tending back at home. I felt as if I would be torn asunder.

"Lord, what should I do??"

Waves of past Scripture memorization started crashing into the frayed feelings.

"Rejoice ALWAYS.

Pray CONTINUALLY.

Give thanks in ALL circumstances.

FOR THIS IS GOD'S WILL FOR YOU IN CHRIST JESUS."

1 Thessalonians 5:18 NIV

I received it into my mind, and had to purely trust. Could I be humble enough to reject what my brain was screaming at me? Could I simply receive what God's Word was telling me instead?

I told myself with Holy Spirit-empowered resolve,

*"I **will** rejoice in this opportunity. I **will** rejoice that I have a husband willing to shoulder all the responsibilities. I **will** rejoice that God is able to take care of my family when I am away. I **will** give thanks that this can happen. I will be fully present in each and every moment of this trip. I can do this in confidence that, more than if we are making the right decision or not, it is GOD'S WILL for me to be fully present and fully thankful during this time".*

I *had* to stay there mentally. Otherwise the torment of anxiety would threaten to rip me apart.

Well, as my sweet husband drove me to the airport in those dark morning hours, I was able to fully enjoy him. Fully be thankful for all the sacrifices he was making. I could fully receive the gift he was trying to give me. I could rest in the fact I could only be in one place at one time and God was the only one that could be in all the places that my mind would want to worry about.

As we pulled up to the terminal, I hugged and kissed that amazing husband. I cuddled my three-year-old in the car for a few minutes and told him how much fun he would have with his Daddy that week. I strapped my infant to myself and started wheeling my luggage away from their loving gaze. As I walked into the airport, the doors closed behind me. And so did the doors to the hurry scurry that I was emerging from.

As I entered, clear instructions came.

"Detox from the doing."

I had written out all the things I needed to accomplish in the nooks and crannies of traveling: emails to teachers, finishing writing the birthday cards that were now late, tending to my part-time business details, schedule my client calls, follow up on bank statements.

But instead, I was to *detox from the doing.*

So that day, as my baby daughter and I dealt with security lines, plane rides, layovers, and more plane rides, I treated it all like I was doing it with Jesus as my faithful companion. I put down the relentless to-do lists that hounded me and had become my replacement companion (to Jesus) in the weeks and months leading up to this. I fought the urge to "just get this quick thing done." We went slowly. I stopped constantly checking my phone I talked to Jesus and He fellowshipped with me. Mid-escalator ride, He plopped "1 Peter 3" into my mind. I resolved to look it up on the airplane. His Presence and the peace He brings started soothing my soul, WHILE I was navigating the airport.

I was experiencing the climax of humility.

Peace was not necessarily getting away from my life, but taking the lower position IN my life so that His presence could flood all the places I found myself.

Andrew Murray says it in the last chapter of his book,

"The highest glory of the creature is in only being a vessel – to receive and enjoy and show forth the glory of God. It can do this only as it is willing to be nothing in itself, that God may be all.

Water fills first the lowest places.

The lower, the emptier, a man lies before God, the speedier and fuller will be the inflow of the Divine Glory." (Chapter 12, pg 40)

And this was it: the flow of the Divine Glory into "real" life. The fullness of heaven available to me, even IN me, whether I was riding an escalator or surrounded by all the logistics of nine children. Humility leads to trust and trust leads to surrender of control (and anxiety). Today it was in trusting the Father, that I could *entrust* all the details to the father of my kids while I was gone. Trust was the humbling that allowed me to fully be present in all that God had in store for me.

And it was peace.

I sat in a cramped airplane, while occupying a busy six-month-old. I got my faded travel Bible out and tucked it into the seat pocket in front of me. I planned to look up the 1 Peter 3 passage as soon as the squirming little daughter of mine fell asleep.

Eventually I was able to sneak some moments of quiet reading. If the early morning reminder wasn't enough, the Lord was confirming it once again – the freedom and beauty that comes with submission, the peace that accompanies the humility to submit. This time, it wasn't just to God, but the people God puts in our lives, like my loving husband.

*"Wives, in the same way submit yourselves to your own husbands...Your beauty should come from your inner self, the unfading beauty of a gentle and quiet spirit, which is of great worth in God's sight. For this is the way the holy women of the past who put their hope in God used to adorn themselves. **They submitted themselves** to their own husbands....**and (did) not give way to fear.**" Peter 3:1-5*

I read the passage, and tears welled up in my eyes as I received the message once again.

"Trust Me, trust your husband. And go with thanksgiving in your heart."

There. There it was again. Humility as the antidote to anxiety. Submission as the means to usurping fear. As I submitted to God and to my husband, I could experience the way in which surrender provides the way out from "giving in to fear".

The fading New England light streamed through the glass windows. On the walls hung pictures of all the memories of a life richly lived for God and others. My baby daughter sat on the lap of my seasoned friend. Her wrinkled-from-a-full-life fingers played across the piano keys. Beautiful melodies floated through the air.

We had just finished a home-cooked meal of vegetables and soup and homemade muffins laid out on a tablecloth with napkin rings and delicately rolled cloth napkins. The joyous reunion with my dear friends had led to rich dinner conversation full of life stories and testimonies of God's work. Our intertwined hearts had been woven together years prior during our urban church planting endeavors and weekly prayer meetings. I experienced a "coming home" feeling as our hearts for the Lord and each other were reignited over our dinner conversation. We were full – full of nourishing food and full of nourishment for the soul.

The tidy, cozy room spotted with antiques enveloped me in an embrace of nurture and comfort. Years before, it was moments like these, at my own grandmother's house, that had fueled the first book I wrote. Here I was, trying to finish my second book, and I found myself in the exact scene that I needed to do so. This was the exact moment I had been longing for. And only my Heavenly Father had seen the yearning….

Two weeks prior, on a very full Saturday, I was pushing through the week's exhaustion in order to get everybody where they needed to be, doing what they needed to be doing. Hosting a birthday party for my preteen, getting children to their appointments, showing up for a friend's birthday party, taking girls shopping for homecoming dresses, all while stopping to nurse my baby in the in between moments. And I was spent. As I drove, quiet tears escalated while I blasted the children's songs to mask the sobbing. I had felt so raw, always pouring out for my children but longing to feel nurtured and supported myself. Having lost my mother to cancer as a teen and my grandmother to a stroke as an adult, it felt disorienting to be in such a nurturing and caretaking role without the backbone of the older generations to fall back on. Ever since this new ninth baby had been born, I had longed for a little respite of being nurtured and poured into by another nurturer. Simply put, I missed my mom and grandma.

But in that moment while melodies played through the sunbeams, I felt as if I could have been sitting in my grandmother's living room, six years and three children ago. It was the exact scenario my heart had been aching for on that frantic Saturday. The longing to belong, to feel nurtured, to be cared for and to know I was enjoyed by another was occurring. Despite not having the biological nurture of my maternal support system, I was experiencing it through the Bigness of God as He manifests it through His people, His Body.

The relationships, the meal, the music, the sunbeams bathed my soul in warmth. Every fiber of my being absorbed the moment.

I was in awe.

Tears welled up as I relished the way my Heavenly Father was meeting me in the most intimate of ways – ways I would have missed had the antidote to anxiety not won out in that early morning battle to submit to my husband and trust my Lord. God had seen the tears the weeks prior. He had heard the cries. He had seen the ache of longing in my heart.

And He was answering me.

This journey of humbling myself before the Lord of All had not resulted in my personhood ending up in obscurity, but rather my personhood being met in the most intimate of ways. God was putting on display how intricately He knew me, saw me, and delighted to grant me the desires of my heart.

I was experiencing the fruit of humility as promised in Scripture.

"Humble yourselves before the Lord, and He will lift you up in honor."
James 4:10 NLT

It wasn't the lifting up and honoring to gain the applause and recognition of people. No, that would never have satisfied my deepest desires. The honoring I was experiencing was the honor of being *known*. How could it be that the God of the entire universe, Who orchestrates the orbiting of planets in their galaxies as well as the tiniest moments of mankind, had coordinated that exact experience? How many more billions of circumstances and scenarios was He also coordinating for individuals around the world who call Him Father? How could He be so vast but also so intimate?

As I had lowered myself to behold Him more fully, He had honored me. He had lifted me up as a beloved object of His affection, by meeting me in the most sacred of spaces and deepest of desires.

God's invitation, Murray's invitation, to desire "to be nothing in myself, so that God can be all and meet all needs" is not an invitation into obscurity but into intimacy.

An intimacy that is the antidote to anxiety.

EPILOGUE

Dear Reader, there is no formula. As the queen of self-help books, new strategies and attempts at implementing systems, I know how frustrating it can be to not have a tried-and-true system to get out of unpleasant circumstances. If you've read this far, you have seen an even greater reality unfold throughout the stories on these pages.

Instead, I would imagine Jesus saying to you,

"There is no formula. If there was, you wouldn't need ME.

I offer no systems, just an invitation into intimacy.

Come, allow all the pressure you face,

internally and externally,

to press you into my warm embrace of love and friendship.

I was crucified so that I could give you this access

to *Me*."

Made in the USA
Columbia, SC
24 June 2024

37579075R00088